From Sake to Soy,
Essential Ingredients for
Japanese Home Cooking

The JAPANESE PANTRY

EMIKO DAVIES

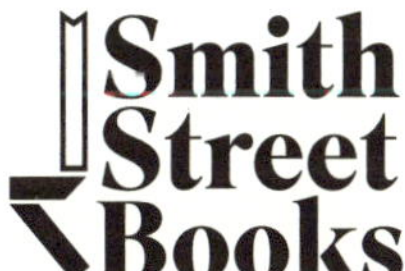

Smith Street Books

CONTENTS

Building my own Japanese pantry

I was inspired to write this book after the release of my previous cookbook, *Gohan*, in which I wrote about the Japanese home cooking that I grew up with, as the daughter of a Japanese mother who happens to be a wonderful home cook.

My mother is one of those cooks who can just open a fridge and, even if there doesn't appear to be anything interesting in it, can create a delicious meal out of seemingly thin air. She never follows a recipe and doesn't usually purposefully plan out meals. She's a very instinctive cook, like my obaachan (grandmother), following appetites and the season, using what she has. And what she always had, no matter where we lived while I was growing up between Australia and China, was an arsenal of Japanese ingredients in the pantry that she could reach for in an instant.

This is home cooking. And this is how I learned how to cook, too. When I grew up and went off to university on the East Coast of the United States and eventually moved to Italy, I would seek out a few Japanese ingredients to have in my tiny kitchens so that I always had the flavours of the home that I missed.

Soy sauce was the first thing I would look for, along with Japanese rice. Then I began to add mirin, a container of miso, sake if I could find it. My mother sometimes sent me some nori to rip into pieces and pick up rice or wrap around onigiri; or a range of teas, the aroma of which would transport me immediately into my grandparents' living room in Chiba, just outside Tokyo. Slowly and surely my arsenal grew.

It turns out that, even in the small Tuscan village where I now live (a place where it is notoriously difficult to eat anything other than Tuscan food), Japanese home cooking is absolutely doable. In fact, it is completely achievable anywhere. It is getting easier and easier to buy good-quality Japanese ingredients online. Japanese cooking relies first and foremost on good local peak-season ingredients. When you start with that and then add a few everyday but umami-rich pantry ingredients, together with some basics such as rice and noodles, you are never far away from creating a deliciously effortless meal.

There are seven chapters in this book, organised by ingredient – soy sauce, miso, seaweed, sake, rice vinegar, sesame and tea. These are what I consider essential in my own pantry for making a huge variety of my favourite Japanese dishes, both sweet and savoury. They are, however, by no means exhaustive and I mention many others throughout the book. (Katsuobushi gets a special mention, for example.)

Every single one of these essential everyday ingredients also happens to be nutrition packed and many are now considered 'super foods', backed by science. But, to my Japanese ancestors, it was just part of the ancient knowledge that eating these things made you not only feel good but played an important part in contributing to a long, healthy life.

I should point out that, along with seaweed, three ingredients in particular are the pillars of Japanese cuisine – soy sauce, miso, sake. They all have something very important in common: these are fermented ingredients, born from a special mould called koji. As chefs René Redzepi and David Zilber write in the *Noma Guide to Fermentation*, koji is 'indistinguishable from magic'. It plays such an important part that it would not be exaggerating to say Japanese cuisine and Japanese culture would not be what they are today without koji. These centuries-old koji-fermented condiments are still at the heart and soul of Japanese home cooking.

Until the Second World War many of these koji-based ingredients were still produced in a way that would today be considered artisanal – by hand, with little reliance on machines, using wild yeasts and wooden tools. It was quite common for people to make their own miso at home; imagine the variety of flavours. Almost all these everyday ingredients are now produced industrially, meaning some of that flavour has been standardised, but they are now accessible around the world and recipes can be easily replicated everywhere.

You might notice that these koji condiments are frequently used in combination (and that many recipes could arguably belong in more than one chapter). In particular, the trio of soy sauce, mirin and sake create a balanced base for soups, marinades and sauces. Soy sauce is there for savouriness, mirin for sweetness and sake for umami. Then, depending on the dish, there might be a splash of rice vinegar for gentle acidity, a spoonful of miso for deep flavour, or perhaps the ultimate umami backbone – dashi made from kombu kelp. Maybe some sesame seeds to garnish, or sesame oil for a touch of earthiness.

Cooking with these ingredients is a delicate balancing act of flavours, but, once you understand how they work together, you won't even need to look at the recipes and you'll be cooking like my mother – *a bit of this and a bit of that, a taste and then a bit more of that.*

I hope you will be inspired by how approachable and simple Japanese home cooking can be – not to mention, quick, economical, nourishing, comforting and flavourful – once you have some staple ingredients at your fingertips. As Japanese food writer, and Head of Osaka's Culinary Institute, Shizuo Tsuji wrote in *Japanese Cooking: A Simple Art*: 'As long as you know the rules, and know what authentic Japanese food is, there is almost no limit to the variations you can make with local ingredients.'

さしすせそ

Sa Shi Su Se So

One way to remember some of the essential flavours of Japanese home cooking is to know the five 's' sounds of the Japanese alphabet: sa; shi; su; se; so (さ – し – す – せ – そ). This widely known mnemonic explains some of the most important flavours in a nutshell.

Sa stands for *sato*, the word for sugar. Sweetness is always important to balance out the saltier flavours in Japanese cooking that come from soy sauce and miso. Most commonly, sugar is used, but also mirin or honey for a more subtle kind of sweetness. My preference is always raw (demerara) sugar, because it has a nuttier, caramel flavour and tends not to be oversweet. I also like Okinawan black sugar, which is incredibly nutritious with almost balsamic, molasses-like flavours. It is darker, though, so will affect the colour of the dish. You can also use soft brown sugar for deeper flavour.

Shi stands for *shio*, which means salt. It's quite self-explanatory, but often I don't use much salt when I'm cooking Japanese food, because of the other sources such as soy sauce and miso. Salt is also useful in pickling, to draw out moisture from vegetables before marinating, or for firming up fish before cooking. Moshio is an ancient Japanese salt made from deep seawater and seaweed that makes a delicious finishing salt. Otherwise use sea salt.

Su stands for, well, *su*, which means vinegar. Rice vinegar is important for preserving foods, from sushi rice to pickles to marinades that make food last longer. Japanese rice vinegar is unique in that it is already a balance of slightly sweet, mellow acidity.

Se stands for soy sauce – if you use the old spelling, *seuyu*, instead of today's shoyu. Japanese cuisine wouldn't be what it is today without this sauce made of fermented soybeans, wheat and salt. It is not only a dipping sauce, but a marinade, a pickling liquid and much more.

So stands for miso, one of the most unique flavours of Japanese cuisine. Earthy and full of umami, it is often used in combination with dashi (page 108–9) for soup or with some sweetness from sugar or mirin to balance out the saltiness in sauces; or, more rarely, with rice vinegar, for example in nuta (page 188).

麹、日本の国菌

Koji, the national fungus of Japan

Fungi (yeasts and moulds) have played an important role in world cultures since ancient times to ferment and preserve foods – think of bread, cheese, cured meats, wine, beer, even cocoa, for example. But koji is unique to Japanese cuisine and it is koji mould that has done the heavy lifting in the country's fermented foods for the past 2000 years. We really cannot discuss Japanese cuisine without looking at the role of koji – Japan's 'national fungus', as it has been dubbed by the Brewing Society of Japan.

Koji is what gives Japanese food its distinct flavour; it is essential in the production of the most important Japanese ingredients, such as soy sauce and miso, and alcoholic preparations such as mirin, sake (and, by extension, rice vinegar) and shochu, the distilled spirit that is made from a variety of local ingredients, including rice, sweet potatoes and buckwheat. Like the yeast starter in bread-making or malt in beer-brewing, koji is what kickstarts the process of fermentation.

'Japanese food would be unrecognisable without koji – there would be no sake, soy sauce, miso or rice vinegar,' writes Nakaji-san in his book *Koji for Life*. He goes on: 'Sake is made from rice and koji, and deeply intertwined with the concept of Japanese religion, which in turn led to the development of traditional performing arts and music. So, you could say that the whole of Japanese culture has been nurtured by koji.'

Technically speaking, 'koji' refers to the preparation of steamed soybeans, rice or other grains, such as wheat and barley, inoculated with koji-kin or koji mould (*Aspergillus oryzae*). When koji is mixed with rice, you can make sake; from that sake, when it's combined with acetic bacteria, you get rice vinegar. When you mix koji with soybeans and toasted, crushed wheat and salt, you get soy sauce; mix it with rice or barley, mashed soybeans and salt, you have miso. These are unmistakably, uniquely Japanese ingredients. 'When Japanese people travel, many start craving these flavours of "home", exposing their intimate connection to koji,' writes Nakaji-san.

Making koji involves perfectly steaming rice (or other grains or soybeans) and inoculating it evenly with the koji-kin, then leaving in a warm, humid place for about 48 hours. Although koji is now, thanks to technology, usually made in carefully controlled environments, Japan's humid summer climate was already ideal for this process. Around the 12-hour mark some of the rice will start showing growth of mycelia and take on a distinct sweet aroma. By 36 hours koji begins to produce enzymes. At 48 hours the rice should have a characteristic fluffy, bloomy, white mycelia coating and a nutty aroma of chestnuts, signifying it is ready to use. It can be used immediately to make miso, for example, or dried or frozen for later.

The kanji characters for koji are either 麹 or 糀 and both ideograms tell us about the process of koji-making. The first kanji character is borrowed from Chinese and contains the radicals for barley on the left and, on the right, rice being 'wrapped'. The second character is a Japanese invention and is made up of the radicals for rice on the left and flower on the right – as watching koji bloom can be likened to a flower blooming. It's interesting to note that the koji that developed in Japan is a different strain from the one that developed in China and other Asian countries, meaning Japanese koji is truly unique.

What makes koji such an important ingredient in the making of delicious fermented foods is its ability to create a variety of enzymes. 'These enzymes break down the grain and koji digests the resulting molecules to keep growing. Take rice koji, for example. When given optimum temperature and moisture, koji grows mycelia around and into steamed rice and produces plenty of enzymes,' writes Nakaji. It is these enzymes that produce all the sweetness and umami in these condiments that give us the flavours that add 'joy to life', as Nakaji says.

There are about 100 different kinds of these enzymes – the exact number is unknown as new koji enzymes are discovered constantly. They include amylases, which transform starch into sugar, and proteases, which break down proteins into amino acids, which equates to umami. This balance of koji enzymes creates a product that has not only the complex savoury flavours associated with umami, but also colour, aroma, nutrients and vitamins. A skilled koji-maker can control the enzymes by controlling the temperature during the last phase of koji-making – a sweeter koji is obtained by increasing the temperature slightly, while a more umami-rich koji can be achieved by maintaining the temperature.

Today you can easily buy koji online, usually in a dried form so it is transportable and keeps well. In Japan about ten producers of koji spores supply the 3000-plus businesses that make fermented foods. These koji producers, known as moyashi-ya, have been doing this for at least 500 years, passing on and keeping alive this valuable fungus for generations. A small but growing number of people are learning how to make it themselves at home – there is a new revolution of koji gurus who teach others how to make and use it. Nakaji-san is one such teacher and I highly recommend his charming and accessible book, *Koji for Life*, written in both English and Japanese.

肉食忌避の歴史

The taboo of eating meat in Japan

Religion has had a great influence on the cuisine of Japan. For roughly 1200 years, from 675 to 1872, in line with both Buddhism and Shintoism, it was forbidden to kill animals and taboo to eat meat. There were exceptions, including fish and sea creatures (not banned in Shintoism), birds (sacred in Shintoism but acceptable as food in Buddhism), or even wild animals that were occasionally hunted for medicinal purposes (it was said that wild boar had restorative powers) or because they threatened farmers' crops (and then you would not let that animal go to waste). But most people had never tasted meat.

Europeans who visited Japan in the 16th century were frustrated at the lack of meat. The missionary Francis Xavier, who led the first Portuguese mission to Japan in 1549, initially respected the meat-eating taboo and abstained, but he was eventually successful in converting many southern Japanese lords to Christianity and they introduced beef and pork to their domains until Christianity was stamped out. The daimyo Toyotomi Hideyoshi questioned the missionaries harshly about eating beef and horse, two animals that were so useful that it was unthinkable to eat them.

The Florentine merchant Francesco Carletti, visiting in 1597, wrote an account noting cows were only used for carrying wood rather than for meat or milk and that drinking milk in particular was greatly frowned upon, 'feeling for it some disgust that we should feel upon drinking fresh blood'. He was annoyed at not being able to find red meat: 'They eat meat very little because of a certain superstition of theirs' (the 'superstition' being Buddhist law), but he was able to hunt birds to satisfy his cravings and seemed pleased at the abundance of thrushes, pheasants and 'turtledoves like ours of exquisite goodness'.

There is a very small section on 'land animals' in the *Ryori Monogatari* of 1643, the oldest Japanese cookbook, suggesting ways to cook animals such as deer, wild boar (which Carletti tried and claimed to be inedible), hare, tanuki (raccoon dogs), river otters and bear. Rather than give recipes, however, this part of the book simply lists the ways they could be prepared, for example, in miso soup, as a suimono (clear soup) or dengaku (grilled with miso paste). It is quite clear that farmed animals are missing and eating animals was an exception.

Author Zenjiro Watanabe explains: 'At the root of the revulsion at the eating of meat was not only the idea that it was unclean, but also Buddhist teachings that prohibited the useless destruction of life. Until fairly recent times, the Japanese had not killed any living creature indiscriminately. In fact, until the 19th century, Japan was the only nation in the world where not a single indigenous species had become extinct. Even those such as hunters, fishermen, and restaurant owners whose profession demanded the killing of animals mourned the loss of life and held memorial services for the animals they killed.'

Wanting to modernise the country and being afraid of falling behind western nations, Emperor Meiji essentially forced the Japanese to begin eating meat in 1872, but the transition was not easy. Even 150 years later, Buddhist priests (like my grandfather) regularly hold special prayer services on behalf of the local butchers to mourn the animals that died.

As evidence that meat is still not central to Japanese cooking, Watanabe points out that you don't see the variety of offal found in Europe. The development of a meat-eating culture is traditionally measured by how completely the animals are used in cooking. Based upon this rule of measure, it is clear that the Japanese are not, even today, true meat eaters. Japan can be considered a fish-eating culture given the fact that every part of the fish, from the head to the intestines, is eaten.

Even now, you will see a Japanese meal is made up of a variety of balanced foods, with meat not necessarily the main ingredient. The nutrients often come from plant-based sources such as tofu (or other soybean ingredients such as miso), sesame, seaweed and even rice.

Geographically, Japan's landscape could never (and still cannot) sustain a meat-eating culture of domesticated livestock like that of Europe, where much farming is to produce feed for animals and the people rely on the livestock for their products (dairy and meat) as food. Three-quarters of Japan is mountains and what little arable land there is is mainly for rice paddies and vegetables. It is the lengthy coastline and surrounding waters that have long supplied the most historically important protein in the Japanese diet: fish.

The way the Japanese have been eating for the past 2000 years is not only self-sufficient and sustainable but, today, would be considered an ideal way to eat for the planet and for health. That said, for the first time in history, meat consumption has just surpassed that of fish in Japan, although it is still only half the amount of countries such as Italy and the United Kingdom and one third the average consumption of the US or Australia, according to the UN's Food and Agriculture Organization.

My grandmother would say, 'you should eat only what you can catch in your hands', such as small fish and shellfish. My mother recalls this was something she read in the philosopher Ekken Kaibara's *Yojokun* (*Instructions for keeping healthy*, 1713). What she cooked regularly and served at her table was mostly seasonal vegetables, rice, eggs, fish, seaweed and plenty of tofu. (Her street, which had a high number of temples, had many fresh tofu shops to service them.) On certain occasions, such as our annual visits to Japan, she would cook meat.

The recipes in this book reflect this flexitarian tradition and the spirit of ishoku dogen: 'food is medicine' (page 155). ●

The extended pantry

ADZUKI BEANS

These small dried red beans don't need soaking before cooking and are almost always eaten sweet, rather than savoury. They are a must if you are planning to make (my favourite) anko for many of the Japanese sweets in this book.

HOBA LEAF

Hoba is a magnolia leaf that you can find dried for culinary use in dishes such as hoba miso (page 86). They add a wonderful aroma. Like persimmon leaves, hoba are used for transporting or wrapping food but not eaten.

JAPANESE RICE

This short-grain rice is its own cultivar (*japonica*) and is vital for Japanese dishes. The grain is almost completely round and it produces a glistening, subtly sticky rice that is easy to eat with chopsticks. You will often find it called by the very general 'sushi rice' or koshihikari, which is a cultivar of *japonica* that is generally considered the very best Japanese rice. See page 36 for how to cook the perfect bowl of rice.

KATAKURIKO STARCH

Traditional katakuriko is a starch made from the roots of the dogtooth violet (a member of the lily family); however, katakuriko is often now made with cheaper, readily available potatoes. It's used for thickening sauces and making crisp fried foods, but you can use regular potato starch instead.

KATSUOBUSHI

These fine, feathery flakes of fermented smoked bonito (skipjack tuna) are vital for adding smoky umami flavour to dashi or as a topping for tofu, noodles, miso soup or vegetable side dishes. See page 111 for more.

KINAKO

This caramel-coloured powder is made from roasted soybeans. It has a naturally sweet, nutty flavour that makes it wonderful in desserts such as matcha jelly (page 128) or for baking. You can also sprinkle it over skewers of sweet dango (page 259).

KOJI

Koji can be found in the form of dried koji rice for making your own miso or sake at home. See page 8 for more.

KONNYAKU

Also known as konjac, this dark grey jelly (dark because it also contains hijiki seaweed) is made from the bulb of the subtropical plant *Amorphophallus konjac* (known by these unappealing names in English: devil's tongue, voodoo lily, snake palm). It's vegan and gluten free and is considered a great health food – it is high in fibre and very good for digestion. You can also find konnyaku in white noodle form, known as shirataki. It is shelf stable until opened; after that, keep in the fridge.

KUZU (KUDZU)

This chunky, white starch comes from the hardy wild kudzu vine (*Pueraria montana var. lobata*) and, like katakuriko starch, it is a very good thickener that is often used in Japanese sweets. It also has properties that make it an important medicinal plant in Japan. Stirring kuzu into a thick 'tea' is a popular cold remedy.

MOCHI BLOCKS (KIRIMOCHI)

These hard dried rice cakes are extremely long lasting – perfect to stash in the pantry. Samurai would carry them as a staple food for the battlefield. When grilled, mochi blocks puff up so they are browned and toasted on the outside but soft and chewy inside. Dipped in soy sauce and wrapped in nori, they make a delicious snack. They're a must in ozoni, a special New Year soup (page 146).

NOODLES

I always have a selection of dried noodles in the pantry. Somen are thin wheat flour noodles that are especially good chilled in the summer. Soba are buckwheat noodles that hold their shape well and are delicious cold in hiyashi soba (page 38). Udon are thick, chewy wheat flour noodles that can be found dried, fresh (vacuum sealed and shelf stable) or frozen. The vacuum-packed ones are my least favourite of the options.

OKINAWAN BLACK SUGAR (KOKUTO)

Black sugar has been made in Okinawa since the 17th century, by boiling down pure cane sugar juice until very dark. It is sold in large chunks, rather than powder. Black sugar has a rich, molasses-like flavour, almost balsamic. It is made into a syrup called kuromitsu and can be used in place of regular sugar. It is not as refined as white and brown sugar, so is rich in minerals such as potassium and iron – it's seen as an excellent pick-me-up if you're unwell.

SANSHO PEPPER

The Japanese pepper tree, or Japanese prickly-ash, a small spiny citrus tree, is native to Japan. One of the great things about planting your own tree (other than the fact that butterflies love it) is you can use both the leaves (known as kinome) and the peppercorns in dishes such as kabayaki sardines (page 44). The pepper has a distinct spicy citrus flavour and is a close relative of Sichuan pepper (although without the numbing properties). It is one of the important spices in shichimi togarashi.

SHICHIMI TOGARASHI

This mild Japanese spice mix means 'seven spices' and is used to add a bit of heat to noodles and other dishes. It dates back to the 17th century and includes ground chilli, sansho (Japanese pepper), sesame, citrus rind, ginger and nori.

SHIITAKE MUSHROOMS

Dried shiitakes are one of the best things to have in your pantry. Like katsuobushi and kombu, they are full of umami and can be added to stock for an instant boost of flavour for noodles and soups. They can be used in place of katsuobushi to make a vegan dashi.

SHIRATAMAKO FLOUR

This glutinous rice flour might be a little harder to find, but it is worth it. Rather than a fine powdery flour, it comes in the form of crumbly, chunky granules and is used for making mochi desserts such as matcha mochi crepes (page 256) and dango (page 259). It gives them the characteristic mochi chew.

UMEBOSHI

Salt-pickled unripe Japanese ume plums are partially sun-dried before going into a jar with a few leaves of red shiso for colouring. They have a pronounced salty–sour flavour and are a staple in Japanese households. Umeboshi last for years and are considered a natural health remedy. You eat them simply with rice, but try umeboshi-braised chicken (page 152) and irizake (page 142), a lip-smacking dressing that you will want to put on everything.

UMESHU

Another use for little sour green ume plums is to make a deliciously fragrant liqueur. Shochu, sugar and plums are soaked together for three months, then strained and, if necessary, diluted slightly to make this sweet liqueur that can be served over ice or topped up with sparkling water. Try it in a sake sour cocktail (page 164).

WASABI

This green rhizome grows in clear mountain streams; Shizuoka is particularly famous for it. Fresh wasabi (*Wasabia japonica*) is traditionally grated on shark-skin graters only when it is needed, as it loses flavour within minutes.
It has a sharp heat but smooth, long-lasting flavour, a world apart from so-called wasabi in a tube – even the best quality of which is often made with a mixture of horseradish, mustard, starch and food colouring, often without any actual wasabi. That spurt of intense, but short-lived, nose-tingling heat you feel is mustard essence. Look for *hon wasabi* ('real wasabi'), which should contain only grated wasabi and no horseradish, mustard or colourants. Once opened, store in the fridge and consume the small tube as quickly as possible.

YUZU

While fresh yuzu yields notoriously little juice, it's quite convenient to have a bottle of yuzu juice in your pantry for making ponzu sauce (page 42). You can also add its uniquely citrusy but not-too-sour flavour to cocktails or baked goods. If you are lucky enough to have access to a yuzu plant, however, you can try making yubeshi (page 90).

Planning a Japanese meal

The typical Japanese meal can be modelled around the concept of *ichiju-sansai* (一汁三菜), literally 'one soup, three dishes'. A small bowl of rice and a little dish of pickles are already a given in this scenario, to which you would add one soup (typically miso soup, which changes constantly, according to the season) and three other dishes. These would usually consist of a 'main' (perhaps a piece of grilled fish or meat, sashimi or something fried) and two side dishes, which would usually be vegetables – one simmered (nimono), and one dressed in sauce (aemono).

It sounds like a lot of work, but often a number of these dishes, if not all of them, would already be made. My obaachan always had at least a pot of miso soup ready to go, some pickles, and rice in the rice cooker keeping warm.

When putting dishes together for a Japanese meal, also take into consideration: the type of cooking (there is a Japanese saying, 'Eat it raw before all else, then grill it, and boil it last of all'), the flavours, and whether they are seasonal. 'Seasonality' doesn't just mean that you're using the best produce in season; it also means the food is cooked in a way that you feel like eating – for example, on an oppressively humid, hot summer day, you won't feel like eating a rich stew.

You also don't want your meal to be dishes that are all the same type of cooking, but rather a variety – something simmered, something fried or grilled (in fact the Japanese word 'yaki' means both), something blanched or steamed or raw. It is about balance.

While breakfast, lunch and dinner can all look like some version of ichiju-sansai, sometimes, you might just have a big bowl of noodles or a donburi – a large bowl of rice with a topping, like oyakodon (page 32) or chicken teriyaki (page 34). And, when you really don't feel like much at all, there is ochazuke (page 246) or a simple bowl of somen noodles (page 40).

ICHIJU-SANSAI MENU IDEAS

You can choose steamed rice (page 36) or another rice dish such as hijiki onigiri (page 120) or hijiki & mackerel rice (page 124). You are spoiled for choice with pickles. Miso soup ingredients can change according to the season, or try the heartier pork miso soup (page 72) or a clear ozoni (page 146). Here are suggestions for a main and two sides of the 'sansai'.

Miso mackerel (page 88) or umeboshi-braised chicken (page 152)
Wafu salad (page 185)
Spinach with tofu, miso & sesame (page 212)

·

Tsukune chicken meatballs (page 46)
Avocado with sesame dressing (page 210)
Simmered tofu (page 112)

·

Ginger pork (page 156)
Summer vegetable tosazuzuke (page 186) or sesame 'tofu' (page 224)
Smashed cucumber salad (page 208)

·

Miso & mushrooms on a magnolia leaf (page 86)
Simmered tofu (page 112)
Nanban pumpkin (page 190)

PICKLES

Soy sauce pickles (page 27)
Miso pickles (page 66)
Sake lees pickles (page 144)
Sweet pickles (page 176)
Pickled Japanese scallion (page 178)
Hama-san's daikon beer pickles (page 180)
Pickled watermelon rind (page 182)

·

ONE-POT MEALS

Chicken & egg donburi (page 32)
Hoto noodle soup (page 80)
Vegetable udon curry (page 82)
Hijiki & mackerel rice (page 124)
Shabu shabu (page 222)

·

PERFECT FOR ONE

Udon in chilled sesame sauce (page 216)
Chilled somen noodles (page 40)
Green tea over rice (page 246)
Tuna tataki (page 43)
Chicken teriyaki donburi (page 34)
Tuna in miso-vinegar (page 188)

·

MEALS FOR SHARING

Fried dumplings (page 76)
Gyoza with sesame sauce (page 218)
Hoto noodle soup (page 80)
Pork & vegetable miso soup (page 72)
Shabu shabu (page 222)
Rice cakes with walnut miso (page 74)

·

MAKE AHEAD

Mapo eggplant (page 85)
Miso mackerel (page 88)
Nanban pumpkin (page 190)
Summer vegetable tosazuzuke (page 186)
Vinegar-braised chicken (page 196)
Sanbaizu bonito (page 198)
Ginger pork (page 156)
Umeboshi-braised chicken (page 152)
Kombu-cured sashimi (page 114)

BEAT THE HEAT

Chilled soba salad (page 38)
Summer vegetable tosazuzuke (page 186)
Smashed cucumber salad (page 208)
Seaweed salad (page 118)
Sesame 'tofu' (page 224)
Chilled somen noodles (page 40)
Udon in chilled sesame sauce (page 216)
Ginger pork (page 156)

·

TO WARM UP

Amazake (page 162)
Matcha (page 240)
Sweet arrowroot tea (page 242)
Pork & vegetable miso soup (page 72)
Hoto noodle soup (page 80)
Vegetable udon curry (page 82)

·

TO GO WITH DRINKS

Sake-steamed clams (page 154)
Tuna in miso-vinegar (page 188)
Miso & green onion sauce (page 68) with raw vegetables to dip
Genmaicha salt (page 248) with edamame
Scallops cooked in butter & sake (page 150)
All the pickles

·

VEGAN HIGHLIGHTS

Hijiki onigiri (page 120)
Sesame 'tofu' (page 224)
Nanban pumpkin (page 190)
Rice cakes with walnut miso (page 74)
Hoto noodle soup (page 80)
Miso & green onion sauce (page 68)
Spinach with tofu, miso & sesame (page 212)
Udon in chilled sesame sauce (page 216)

Cook's notes

KITCHEN EQUIPMENT

You really don't need anything special to make these dishes, but I do mention some traditional Japanese utensils and kitchenware that you might like to know about, plus their substitutes. If you have a sharp knife, you're most of the way there already.

One of my most-used items is a suribachi, a Japanese ceramic bowl with grooves for grinding ingredients (especially sesame), similar to a mortar and pestle.

I also love my oroshigane – a little grater often made of metal but also ceramic (oroshi), that has tiny spikes for grating ginger and daikon. You could use a microplane, but it's not a perfect substitute: the ginger fibres get stuck and the daikon doesn't grate well either. If anything, an oroshigane is one thing I would recommend adding to your kitchen arsenal.

CUP MEASURES & TABLESPOONS

I tested these recipes with a 250 ml (8½ fl oz) cup; please note that US cups are 237 ml (8 fl oz), so American cooks can be generous with their liquid cup measurements. If in doubt, go with the weight measurements.

I also use 20 ml (¾ fl oz) tablespoons. Cooks who use 15 ml (½ fl oz) tablespoons can be generous too; although, saying that, I have been mindful of this tiny 5 ml (¼ fl oz) difference and I would like to assure you that nothing will go wrong if you use your own tablespoons. After all, this is home cooking – you can always taste and adjust to your liking.

OVEN TEMPERATURES

There is not a lot of baking in Japanese recipes because, historically, ovens were not used. Where there is, please note that if you're using a fan-forced oven you may need to decrease the temperature by 20°C (70°F) or reduce the baking time a little.

SALT

In many of these recipes there is enough salt from soy sauce, miso or even umeboshi plums, but salt is important also for drawing out moisture from vegetables or even fish.
I always cook with natural sea salt. If you are using kosher or iodised table salt, you might get slightly different results, so please taste as you go.

Note that you do not need to salt the water for cooking noodles or rice.

SUGAR

There are a lot of sauces, marinades and dressings in this book that require a delicate balance of sweetness. I prefer to use raw (demerara) sugar, which I feel is less cloying, but you can use white granulated sugar or even honey, if you prefer. In this case, taste along the way to make sure that it is balanced for you.

EGGS

Where possible, use free-range organic eggs. I use 55 g (2 oz) eggs, which correspond to 'large' eggs in the US, Canada and Australia, or 'medium' eggs in Europe. Size won't usually matter, but I've specified it when boiling eggs, so you get perfect jammy results for soy-marinated eggs (page 28), for example.

VEGETARIAN & VEGANS

Note that the majority of these recipes are vegetarian and, where they're not, I've given suggestions for variations to easily make them so. Therefore, all the recipes are potentially vegetarian and almost all of them (aside from a handful that include egg and a few shellfish dishes) vegan. For example, the tonjiru (a hearty pork and vegetable miso soup, page 72) is brilliant without the pork and the kombu-cured sashimi (page 114) isn't just for sashimi, it's a gamechanger for giving cooked or raw vegetables a umami oomph! Japan is, after all, the home of shojin ryori, Zen Buddhist temple cuisine, which is mostly vegan.

鶴醤

醬油

SOY SAUCE

YAMAROKU
SETOUCHI

醤油
SOY SAUCE

'Just about everything could benefit from a splash of top-shelf shoyu.'

NANCY SINGLETON HACHISU, JAPANESE FOOD AUTHORITY

Soy sauce, or shoyu (醤油), is perhaps one of the most recognisable ingredients in Japanese cooking. It is present in almost everything and holds a permanent place in Japanese food culture, whether it's in a glass bottle on the table at home, or the little plastic fish with red lids in takeaway containers. It is, as Richard Hosking writes in *A Dictionary of Japanese Food*, 'the essential, basic flavourer of Japanese food'. It is unsurprising, then, that this is the largest chapter in this book. However, I think its long history and the process of making this irreplaceable ingredient is very little known to most people, even those who have a bottle in their cupboard. By learning a little more, we can appreciate its versatility in the kitchen – not just for seasoning, but also for marinating, making a variety of sauces, pickling and even using in sweets.

Japanese soy sauce is usually made from three ingredients: soybeans, wheat and salt. Four, if you count water. Originally from China, soy sauce was invented around the third century BC (although some believe it was earlier, making it potentially the oldest condiment in history). It was developed to preserve protein-rich foods and to 'stretch' salt, which was an expensive commodity in ancient times. In its first form, soy sauce was made with fermented fish (known as gyosho) and would have been not unlike Vietnamese fish sauce, but, when it was introduced to Japan in the seventh century, it was brought by Buddhist monks, who had developed a vegetarian version of gyosho, replacing the fish with soybeans.

Japanese soy sauce developed into its own entirely unique product over the centuries, distinct from those of neighbouring countries such as China and Korea. Today, you simply cannot substitute another style of soy sauce for Japanese soy sauce, if you want the authentic flavour of Japanese dishes.

The process of making soy sauce can take many months (years, for artisanal brewers). Most soy sauce is made by a method known as honjozo (本醸造), meaning it is completely fermented. A mixture of roasted wheat and steamed or boiled soybeans, known as moromi, is inoculated with koji mould. The moromi mixture then goes into a salt brine to brew, traditionally in wooden barrels or, in modern times, stainless steel tanks. This is usually fermented for six to eight months (longer for artisanal soy sauce) and is then pressed through fine cloth to separate the solids. The resulting soy sauce can be pasteurised by heating and then filtered before bottling or aging.

Interestingly, the process of making soy sauce is often referred to as 'brewing' and soy sauce makers as 'brewers' – if you are familiar with the process of brewing beer, you might think of koji as the substitute for malt.

Soy sauce-making in Japan began to change after the Second World War, when the government required makers to modernise processes in an effort to boost the economy. Enormous stainless steel vats replaced the wooden barrels and fermentation time was cut to a fraction of what it had been. But then, in the 1990s, the country's economy took a turn for the worse and industries across the board found themselves having to cut corners. According to Masakazu Nakai, the eighth-generation owner of Marunaka Shoyu, a 200-year-old soy sauce brewery near Lake Biwa in Shiga prefecture in central Japan, the introduction of modern machinery meant the brewing period became shorter, and cheaper raw materials were imported to cut costs.

Like so many things that changed once mass production took over, this meant that soy sauce became cheaper but not as good as it had been previously, when made by hand with time and passion. Nakai himself was working at a leading soy sauce manufacturer at the time. 'It wasn't long,' he shares, 'before I began to develop a sense of uneasiness. Was this even soy sauce? The lack of human involvement, the lifeless machines, the inert stainless steel barrels... all of these had me questioning my own choices and career path. I consistently found my mind wandering back to my childhood spent in the Marunaka Shoyu brewery, where the brewing craftsman worked in tandem with nature, harnessing the power of the koji that had been living [there] for generations.'

There are still a few artisanal brewers who are dedicated to making soy sauce by traditional methods, where everything is done by hand, using wooden barrels and no modern equipment – but only one per cent of the soy sauce produced in Japan is made this way. By knowing how these artisans are keeping the traditional methods alive, you can understand more about how this ingredient is made and how it is supposed to taste.

Marunaka Shoyu is the only brewery in Japan that uses a unique process called *shiotsuri*, or 'salt-hanging'. Hemp bags of salt are hung in the barrels of water so that the salt dissolves slowly, increasing the salt content slowly. The moromi mixture (made from chemical-free soybeans and wheat that have been grown by the same local farmer since 1963) is mixed twice a day with a long wooden paddle called a kaibou. The brewer looks after the moromi like this for three years, while it ferments. Finally, it is pressed and filtered. At Marunaka Shoyu they fill the hemp bags with the moromi and stack them, using natural gravity and the weight of the bags, as well as an extra weight of wood on top, to obtain the soy sauce that will finally be bottled.

Kamebishi Shoyu in eastern Kagawa prefecture specialises in aged soy sauces – brewed in the same samurai house where the family began their business in 1753, eighteen generations ago. They not only make their own koji, but this is the only brewery that ferments the soybeans and wheat on top of woven straw mats, called mushiro, before it goes into century-old cedar barrels. This mushiro method, which follows a 250-year-old recipe, is protected by intangible folk culture status. Even more impressive, however, is that they produce rare bottles of soy sauce that are aged for up to 38 years. You wouldn't ever cook with something this special, but you might enjoy this shoyu with sashimi or even drizzled on perfect, ripe fruit, such as strawberries, mango or figs, which are considered a luxury in Japan.

Determined to experience an artisanal soy sauce brewery in person, I visit Yamaroku Shoyu on Shodoshima (Shodo Island) in the Seto Inland Sea, where Yasuo Yamamoto, a fifth-generation soy sauce brewer, makes barrel-aged soy sauce known as kioke shoyu. He uses cedar barrels that are over 150 years old – they are heavily encrusted with salt, healthy bacteria and fungi that are themselves over a century old.

Open vats of moromi ferment in the workspace at Yamaroku Shoyu, with its earthen floor, mud walls and simple wooden roof. It is like visiting a living museum of microorganisms: there are about 100 varieties of fungi and bacteria living here, in the wood of the enormous cedar barrels, that date back to the Meiji era when the brewing house was built. You can feel that the place is alive. It's a dark, quiet space and the deep aroma of soy sauce infiltrates the air. Fans whir in the background, helping to spread the 'kin', the fungi, and control the temperature, which is not easy to do with wooden barrels, although the particularly warm, dry microclimate of the south side of the island is ideal. 'We could never move from here,' explains one of the staff members

as we admire the thick, fuzzy layers on the barrels' exterior. 'We would lose all of this.' It's the microorganisms living in the brewery that give barrel-aged soy sauce its utterly unique flavour. They are the 'secret ingredient' in every bottle of soy sauce made here.

The barrels – kioke – are two metres tall and can each hold 3600 litres of soy sauce. We climb up a rickety wooden staircase to look into one and find a new batch, made the day before, of moromi mash of soybeans and wheat. It will be left in here to ferment, initially, for a year and a half and then go back into the barrel for a couple more years of aging; this means that those new beans we can see bobbing around in the barrel won't be bottled until four years from now.

These barrels can last for well over a century and were once used for making all fermented products in the country – not only soy sauce, but also sake, mirin, rice vinegar, miso and even pickles. But what happens when the barrels need replacing? As there are fewer and fewer artisanal brewers using kioke – currently only 3000 are used in Japan, while in the 1940s there were a million barrels in use in sake breweries alone – the art of making them was also heading towards extinction. So Yasuo Yamamoto decided to learn how to make them himself from the last kioke-maker in Japan. Losing the kioke would have meant losing the 'main ingredient' of this important Japanese staple. He now leads workshops to teach other brewers how to make their own cedar barrels, keeping this tradition alive.

Each brewery produces a completely different soy sauce; each batch is potentially different. The result is that these soy sauces have far more complex and interesting flavours. 'Even prepared with the same recipe, at the same time, the results are different because the kioke are different,' says Yoko Suzuki from Suzuki Shoyu Ten in Fukushima prefecture.

Artisanal soy sauce from the likes of Yamaroku are available all over the world; you just have to know, firstly, that they exist and, secondly, what to look for. Then you can experience how unique and versatile soy sauce can be – and not only for Japanese dishes. As Japanese food authority Nancy Singleton Hachisu, points out: 'Just about everything could benefit from a splash of top-shelf shoyu.'

I hope that, after cooking your way through this chapter, you will feel confident to explore soy sauce as more than a dipping sauce. Think of having a collection of different types, to match to any particular dish. You can even make your own 'blend', mixing different artisanal soy sauces to obtain the perfect custom flavour for whatever you're cooking.

TYPES OF SOY SAUCE

According to JAS (Japanese Agricultural Standards), there are five types of soy sauce:

Koikuchi (濃口) is often known as a 'dark' soy sauce. Rich in flavour and with a deep colour, this is made with equal quantities of soybeans and wheat. Koikuchi is the most common Japanese soy sauce, accounting for about 80 per cent of the soy sauce produced in Japan – it's likely you have a bottle of this sitting in your pantry right now. It is also the most versatile, so you can use it for cooking or for the table.

Usukuchi (薄口) comes from the Kansai region and is considered a 'light' soy sauce. This can be confusing, as it is lighter in colour and body (*usukuchi* literally it means 'thin taste') but not necessarily in flavour. It is saltier than regular koikuchi, is matured for a shorter time and, because it has less colour, it's most often used for cooking, for example in custards, soup stock or sauces.

Tamari (溜) comes from the Chubu region in central Japan and is made without wheat (so it is often considered gluten free). It is most similar to the ancient version of soy sauce that arrived in Japan in the seventh century and is related to the liquid by-product of miso making (miso damari). Tamari is a full-flavoured, umami-rich soy sauce, best for table use with sushi and sashimi, but also in sauces such as teriyaki.

Shiro (白) or white shoyu, on the other hand, is made with mostly wheat and only a very small amount of soybeans. It is mild and pale (which is why it is called 'white', although it is actually more amber hued) and this is why it is most appreciated – you will find it called for in certain dishes, such as soups, pickles and chawanmushi, as it doesn't change their colour.

Saishikomi (再仕込) is the most luxurious kind of soy sauce – dark, thick, intense. Its name means 'refermented', or twice-brewed, and it originated in Yamaguchi prefecture but today is made by artisans across the country, such as Yamaroku, Suehiro and Kamebishi. Saishikomi requires twice the amount of raw materials and more time to create than other sauces. The shoyu from the first fermentation is mixed again with more soybeans and wheat and can take a further year (or more). You would only use this special soy sauce for the table – with sashimi or chilled tofu, for example.

Keep an eye out also for these two, which can be interesting additions to your pantry:

Marudaizu shoyu, or whole bean soy sauce, is mild yet complex and the ideal condiment for sushi or sashimi.

Kioke shoyu, barrel-aged soy sauce, is an artisanal soy sauce that relies on the use of cedar barrels and the immense variety of fungi and bacteria that inhabit the brewery to create deep, complex flavours.

THE DIFFERENCE BETWEEN EAST ASIAN SOY SAUCES

There are hundreds of soy sauces across the countries of East Asia and their differences in style can be put down to varying brewing methods and ingredients.

Soy sauce from China, its birth place, is called jiang you. It is varied and vast, as you can imagine in such an important regional cuisine. To try to narrow it down succinctly, it is generally only made with soybeans (or perhaps with some wheat flour rather than toasted whole wheat) and has a shorter brewing time. This makes Chinese soy sauce saltier and stronger than Japanese. Ironically, this kind of soy sauce, which is often called 'light' soy sauce is more similar to Japanese 'dark' soy sauce. Chinese 'dark' soy sauce includes sugar or molasses and is an entirely different type of soy sauce – more viscous, to add colour and texture to Chinese dishes. These are the soy sauces that are used mainly for cooking.

Korean soy sauce, or ganjang, is also mostly soybean dominant and is lighter in colour. It is saltier than both Chinese and Japanese soy sauces and most suitable for use in Korean cooking.

It is important to realise that Japanese soy sauce is not easily interchangeable with other soy sauces. It is relatively sweeter – because of the combination of wheat and soy beans (often half and half) – and has a longer brewing time. So, if you are making Japanese food and trying to capture its unique balance of flavours, always use Japanese soy sauce.

HOW TO STORE SOY SAUCE

If you have found yourself a very special artisanal soy sauce, keep it like you would any other precious ingredient, such as olive oil or wine: in a cool, dark place. A refrigerator might be best if you live somewhere very warm. Standard soy sauce can be kept in the pantry but try to ensure it doesn't have big changes in temperature. Soy sauce can develop a strong smell when it is past its prime, so consider buying it in smaller bottles if you don't use it very often – although perhaps this chapter will change your mind.

だし醤油

DASHI SOY SAUCE

DASHI SHOYU

This is a condiment that is often store-bought in Japan, but it is very easy to make at home and will boost the flavour of your soy sauce, whether for cooking or for the table. It is basically a soy sauce infusion of katsuobushi and kombu – a umami bomb, in other words. Use it in place of regular soy sauce for dishes such as soy sauce pickles (opposite), soy-marinated eggs (page 28), chilled somen noodles (page 40), Japanese salad dressings or even hijiki & mackerel rice (page 124). I like to simply make a cold infusion here and keep it in a jar in the fridge.

VARIATION: If you are vegetarian, just leave out the katsuobushi.

MAKES 250 ml (1 cup)

250 ml (1 cup) soy sauce
1 small piece of kombu (about 5 cm/2 in long)
5 g (½ cup) katsuobushi flakes

Pour the soy sauce into a sterilised jar. Add the kombu (cut it with scissors to fit, if necessary) and katsuobushi and leave to infuse overnight in the fridge.

Strain the sauce (you could keep the kombu and katsuobushi to make kombu simmered with soy sauce & mirin (page 110) or add the kombu to soy sauce pickles, opposite).

It's ready to use, or can be stored in the fridge for 3 months.

醤油漬け

SOY SAUCE PICKLES

SHOYUZUKE

Like the other pickles you'll find in this book, you can make this with any seasonal vegetables – chunks of carrot or cucumber, napa cabbage, sliced radish or daikon.

Recently I have become interested in nozawana (野沢菜), a leafy green brassica rapa that is often called Japanese mustard leaf and is related to turnip tops. Nagano prefecture is particularly well known for it. In fact, it takes its name from the hot spring town Nozawa Onsen ('na' simply means vegetable, so 'vegetable from Nozawa'). Turnip seeds from Kyoto were brought here by the head priest of Kenmei-ji temple in the 1700s, but the small turnip that grew from that Kyoto seed became a very different plant in the high-altitude cold climate of Nozawa.

Over the centuries the deliciousness of nozawana has become known all over the country – the first harvest of the young plant is said to be 'tastier than sea bream sashimi' and people still visit the temple to purchase the seeds of the original nozawana when they're harvested in the summer. In November, when the leaves have reached a metre long, the main harvest begins and then so does the pickling.

There are different versions of pickled nozawana, and different family traditions, naturally. Many other dishes are made with these pickles, from onigiri to dumplings and, even when they are overpickled and sour, you can stir-fry or boil them in sake lees – they never get wasted. Nozawana are extremely high in vitamin C.

Although I don't have real nozawana, I make it with their Italian cousin, cime di rapa, or turnip tops. I blanch these first by pouring boiling water over them – in Nozawa Onsen, the vegetables are traditionally washed in the local hot spring waters before being pickled.

Soy sauce pickles are so quick, the pickling liquid is like a salad dressing so you can enjoy them right away or within hours. However, if you can wait a day, these are even better.

FILLS 1 x 250 ml (1 cup) jar

150 g (5½ oz/about 5 stalks) cime di rapa (turnip tops) or Japanese mustard leaf
1 tablespoon soy sauce
1 tablespoon rice vinegar
1 teaspoon sugar
finely sliced chilli, rehydrated kombu or finely chopped ginger (optional)

Cut the cime di rapa stalks and leaves into pieces no longer than 5 cm (2 in). Blanch for 10 seconds in boiling water, then immediately drain in a colander and rinse in cold water. Squeeze as much liquid as you can out of them. Place in a jar, airtight container or resealable plastic bag.

Combine the soy sauce, vinegar and sugar and stir to dissolve the sugar (if you're making a bigger batch, heat in a saucepan to help it along), adding the chilli, kombu or ginger, if you like. Pour over the vegetables. Place a weight on top to keep them submerged in the liquid. (I have pickling weights – but get inventive with food tins if you don't!) If you're using a jar or container, remove the lid and put the weight directly on the vegetables. If you're using a bag, squeeze out the air, seal and place the weight on the bag.

These are best eaten within 3 days, if they last that long.

味玉

SOY-MARINATED EGGS

AJITAMA

Perfect in a bento box, as a snack, in salads, on top of rice or added to a simple bowl of noodles in broth (these are also known as 'ramen eggs'), ajitama look impressive but are actually very easy to prepare. Soft-boiled eggs are simply peeled and marinated in tsuyu sauce (a classic multipurpose sauce made with equal amounts of soy sauce, sake and mirin) for an extra boost of flavour. For a really clean peel, use older rather than the freshest eggs. If I know I'm going to make these, I buy eggs several days in advance.

SERVES 4

2 tablespoons soy sauce
2 tablespoons sake
2 tablespoons mirin
4 eggs (about 55 g/2 oz each)

For the tsuyu, put the soy sauce, sake and mirin in a small saucepan, bring to a lively simmer and cook for about 2 minutes, then leave to cool completely.

In the meantime, bring a small pan of water to the boil and, once simmering, lower the eggs into the water and start timing. Cook for 7 minutes for jammy eggs and 8 minutes for slightly more set eggs. Remove the eggs from the pan immediately and plunge them into cold water to cool down.

Once cool to the touch, crack the eggs all over and peel them gently (it helps to do this under cool water: the water will slip under the skin of the shell and make it easier to remove).

Place the eggs in an airtight container or resealable plastic bag and pour the tsuyu sauce over them. Let them marinate for at least 1 hour and up to 24 hours (longer is better), turning every so often so they are evenly covered in the marinade.

喫茶店の目玉焼き

KISSATEN FRIED EGGS

KISSATEN NO MEDAMAYAKI

The kissaten (喫茶店) is a very special Japanese institution – an old-school coffee shop and tea room. And, by old-school, I mean it will catapult you into the retro Showa era, in terms of atmosphere, furniture, menu, sometimes even the clientele. This is a quiet place to catch up with the community or reflect alone over a cup of coffee and simple breakfast.

On my last visit to Tokyo we came upon an unassuming kissaten (they are almost always unassuming) in Tawaramachi, an equally retro neighbourhood of tidy little streets decorated with tiny pots of plants squeezed into the most unlikely spaces. You'll see Tokyoites riding their bicycles in these backstreets, passing by a mix of old barber shops and repair shops, interspersed with modern coffee shops and juice bars. There were only retirees in the kissaten, which was run by two elderly ladies and offered a simple menu of just a handful of items.

I ordered a cup of coffee and the eggs, which struck me with such nostalgia when I saw them – fried and steamed, perfectly cooked whites with creamy yolks and frilly, crisp, browned bottoms. They were served with a healthy dose of soy sauce, shredded raw cabbage and a huge slab of toasted shokupan – Japanese milk bread – with a knob of butter sliding off it and a small saucer of strawberry jam. If the jam had been honey, I could have been eating at my grandparents' table.

SERVES 1

oil for the pan

2 eggs

splash of soy sauce, finely shredded cabbage, steamed rice or thick buttered shokupan toast with jam or honey, to serve

Heat a lightly greased non-stick pan (I use cast-iron) over medium heat. Crack the eggs into the hot pan.

Add 1 tablespoon water and immediately cover the pan with a tight-fitting lid. Once the top of the egg white is opaque (this can take just 10–20 seconds if the pan is hot enough), remove the lid and continue cooking until the liquid has evaporated and the bottoms are crisp.

Lift carefully onto a plate and serve immediately with your favourite accompaniments – for me the non-negotiable is the soy sauce splashed over the eggs, which are as delicious over steamed rice as they are on thick, buttered toast.

親子丼

CHICKEN & EGG DONBURI

OYAKODON

Oyakodon is one of my ultimate comfort dishes. Oyako means 'mother and child' and don refers to the bowl of rice underneath. These kind of dishes, where a big bowl of steamed rice is topped with something, are called donburi. These are usually served in a large, deep bowl – the sort you might put noodles in, so quite a bit bigger than the little bowls of rice that normally accompany Japanese meals and could fit in the palm of your hand. The key to donburi recipes is the delicious sauce that soaks slowly into the rice beneath, so the dregs in the bottom of the bowl become the best bits.

Like many of the best comfort foods, oyakodon isn't particularly pretty, but don't let that put you off. The succulent pieces of chicken and onion slices are cooked in dashi stock, to which you add soy sauce, mirin and a touch of sugar to make a sweet–savoury sauce. The part I love is the topping – you pour beaten eggs over the top of the saucy chicken and then, once they're cooked but still wobbly, slide this on top of the bowls of rice.

This isn't a particularly old dish – it seems to date to the late 1800s – but there are some modern variations, namely katsudon, which uses breaded pork cutlet (tonkatsu) in place of the chicken. It's a brilliant idea if you have some leftover cotoletta or tonkatsu.

In Japan there are specific pans called oyako nabe that are almost like giant ladles for cooking oyakodon in individual portions, so you don't have to break up the beautiful omelette created by the egg. But you can easily make this in a regular frying pan with a lid.

VARIATION: To make this vegetarian, use mushrooms (king browns, enoki or Swiss brown) instead of chicken.

SERVES 2

1 boneless chicken thigh, cut into chunks
½ onion, thinly sliced
185 ml (¾ cup) dashi (pages 108–9)
2 tablespoons soy sauce (or to taste)
1 tablespoon mirin (or sake)
2 teaspoons sugar
2 eggs, beaten
2 large bowls of steamed rice (page 36), to serve
2 spring onions (scallions), thinly sliced
shichimi togarashi (optional)

Put the chicken, onion, dashi and a pinch of salt in a shallow frying pan (or oyako nabe) and bring to a fast simmer over medium heat. Add the soy sauce, mirin and sugar. Once simmering, it should take about 5 minutes to cook the chicken and soften the onion. Taste and adjust if needed.

While the sauce is simmering, pour over the beaten eggs and place a lid on top. Check after 30 seconds to 1 minute for your ideal wobble – I like it fairly custardy, so I turn off the heat and leave with the lid on while I fill the bowls with rice.

With a ladle, scoop half the chicken and egg onto each bowl of rice, including the pan juices. Top with spring onions and, if you like, a sprinkle of shichimi togarashi.

照り焼きチキン丼

CHICKEN TERIYAKI DONBURI

CHIKIN TERIYAKIDON

This is a delicious one-bowl lunch – and easy to turn into a bento. You can substitute other vegetables for the shishito peppers – try capsicum, stir-fried fresh shiitake mushrooms, your favourite salad leaves, shredded red cabbage or cherry tomatoes.

VARIATIONS: You could also add soy-marinated eggs (page 29) to this. For a vegan version, use firm tofu instead of the chicken and cook in the same way.

SERVES 2

4 boneless chicken thighs
6 shishito peppers
oil for the pan
2 large bowls of steamed rice (page 36), to serve
2 nori sheets

TERIYAKI SAUCE
2 tablespoons soy sauce
2 tablespoons sake
2 tablespoons mirin (or demerara sugar)

Combine the teriyaki sauce ingredients in a bowl, add the chicken and leave to marinate for at least 30 minutes, or overnight if you have time.

Cook the peppers in a hot dry pan (cast-iron is ideal, or, if you have the barbecue going, use that), turning on all sides until blistered and blackened in places. Remove from the pan and keep warm.

Add a touch of oil to the same pan (or barbecue), turn the heat to high and add the drained chicken thighs (keep the marinade – you will need it later). Cook for 3 minutes on each side or until just cooked through. For the last minute, pour on the marinade and let it simmer. If you're using a barbecue, cook the marinade in a pan for about 1 minute, being careful not to let the soy sauce burn – you can also use some of it to baste the chicken.

Remove from the heat. Slice the chicken into thick pieces that are easy to pick up with chopsticks.

To serve, sprinkle a spoonful of warm teriyaki sauce over each rice bowl. Tear up most of the nori sheets into small pieces and sprinkle over the rice, tucking the rest into the side of the bowl. Layer the peppers on one side and, finally, the chicken. Pour on more of the sauce and serve immediately.

ごはんの炊き方

THE PERFECT BOWL OF STEAMED RICE

GOHAN NO TAKIKATA

If you don't have a rice cooker, as I didn't until very recently, here is how to cook perfect Japanese rice on the stovetop. First of all, make sure you are using Japanese rice. It is a special variety called '*japonica*' and is unique: a round, short-grain rice that is glistening, soft, moist and slightly sticky when cooked, making it easy to eat with chopsticks. Soaking the rice for about half an hour before cooking also helps with that soft, sticky consistency.

Koshihikari is a cultivar of *japonica* that is one of the most popular premium rice types. It is cultivated in Niigata prefecture, where it is famous, and in Australia, the United States and Italy. *Japonica* rice is often also labelled 'sushi rice' but it may not be as good quality.

There is a simple, easy ratio to remember: one part rice to one-and-a-half parts water. So, for 1 cup rice, use 1½ cups water. Of course, that ratio will work with anything as the 'cup': a yoghurt pot; a water glass; your favourite teacup …

The traditional Japanese measure is a 'gou' and is equivalent to 180 ml (about ¾ cup). I usually use a standard cup measure, which equals about 200 g (7 oz) of rice.

If you are making donburi, or are simply a rice lover, you will want to double this amount, which makes enough for 3–4 small Japanese rice bowls.

SERVES 3–4

200 g (1 cup) Japanese short-grain rice
375 ml (1½ cups) cool water

Put the rice in a fine-meshed sieve and flush with water under the tap, swirling it with your hand several times. Repeat the washing a couple more times, then put the drained rice in a small heavy-based pan with a tight-fitting lid and add the measured water. Ideally, leave to soak for 30 minutes.

Bring to a simmer over low–medium heat, then cover and turn down the heat to the lowest possible setting. Cook for 10–15 minutes, trying not to take the lid off (if it's your first time using this method, you'll need to keep an eye or an ear on it – you can actually hear when the water has been completely absorbed and you need to take it off the heat so the rice doesn't burn).

Taste the rice: it should be very slightly al dente, soft but not mushy. Take off the heat but keep the lid on and let it finish steaming for another 10 minutes.

夏バテ

Natsubate: Eating to beat the heat in Japan

Unagi – freshwater eel – is a favourite summertime food in Japan and is often eaten for the Day of the Ox (ushi no hi, 丑の日), which falls in midsummer. It is said that eating foods that begin with the letter u – unagi, umeboshi, udon noodles and so on – will help the body ward off heat fatigue, known as natsubate, during the oppressively humid Japanese summers. However, as Yuto Omura recounts on his blog, *Sudachi Recipes*, this might have simply been a clever marketing scheme from a few hundred years ago.

Apparently, during the Edo period, eel was not a popular choice in the summer months because it was out of season and customers considered it too rich a food to enjoy in the heat. So, unagi shops began the tradition of ushi no hi to boost summer sales.

According to author Elizabeth Andoh, however, the first mention of eels as a cure for summer fatigue goes back even further. There appears to also be a poem from the well-regarded anthology known as the *Manyoshu* from 759 that advises anyone feeling unwell in the summer to eat eel.

Perhaps this ancient lore has been around for even longer than we think? The fact is that eels are indeed a very nutritious protein, rich in thiamine (vitamin B), which is said to beat fatigue, as are pork and oily fish such as sardines.

Similarly, ginger pork (page 156) is another favourite dish that is said to help beat fatigue and, if you were to ask my obaachan, she would tell you to eat some pickles – vinegar will help pick you up when you are weary from the heat. ●

冷やし蕎麦

CHILLED SOBA SALAD

HIYASHI SOBA

Japanese summers are oppressive and typical summer meals are designed to help you enjoy cooking and eating, despite the heat. These hiyashi noodles, with their slightly sweet and sour sauce, are a perfect example.

Hiyashi means 'chilled' and this dish is usually prepared with ramen noodles, but any favourite noodle will work: impossibly thin somen; thick and chewy udon; classic ramen. I have even made this with thin angel hair pasta when I didn't have any Japanese noodles on hand – it did the trick!

VARIATIONS: The toppings below are what you'd usually find on hiyashi chuka (the version with chilled ramen noodles), but there are no set rules: open the fridge and see what you have. Consider shredded poached chicken, crab meat or boiled prawns instead of the ham; use soft-boiled eggs or soy-marinated eggs (page 29) if you don't feel like making the omelette strips. Vegans can leave out the ham and anyone might like to add the following: grated carrot; blanched or grilled okra (also said to help in hot weather); thin strips of red or yellow pepper; blanched baby spinach; fresh, shredded shiso leaf.

SERVES 4

2 eggs, beaten
320 g (11½ oz) dried soba noodles
½ cucumber, thinly sliced into finger-length sticks
100 g (3½ oz) cherry tomatoes, halved
4 thin slices roast ham (about 55 g/2 oz), cut into strips
1 spring onion (scallion) or chives, finely chopped
sesame seeds
dash of sesame oil (optional)

SAUCE
80 ml (⅓ cup) soy sauce
2 tablespoons raw (demerara) sugar
2 tablespoons rice vinegar
2 tablespoons water (or dashi)

For the sauce, stir together the ingredients until the sugar dissolves. You can make this in advance and store in the fridge for several days before serving.

Heat a non-stick frying pan over high heat. Pour in half the whisked egg and tilt the pan to make a thin omelette. Cook very lightly for just a minute – don't let it colour. Flip to cook the other side, then turn it out onto a board and cook the remaining egg in the same way. Finely slice into strips.

Cook the noodles according to the packet instructions, then drain and rinse in cold water (this not only cools them down quickly, but also gives the noodles some spring).

Serve the noodles immediately, topped with the cucumber, tomatoes, ham and omelette. Scatter with spring onion and sesame seeds. Each person can pour over some of the sauce, and perhaps a dash of sesame oil, and enjoy immediately.

そうめん

CHILLED SOMEN NOODLES

SOMEN

Impossibly thin somen noodles with umami-packed mentsuyu sauce and a few simple garnishes are so easy to slurp up – just what you need when you're hot and tired in the summertime and can manage only the bare minimum.

You'll often find this served 'buffet style', where you choose your favourite garnishes from little bowls. This is a nice idea if you're serving guests – place the sauce in small bowls on the table with a variety of garnishes, such as those suggested below. All that's left to do is boil the noodles.

To eat, guests add their chosen garnishes to their individual sauce bowl, dip some noodles into the sauce and slurp – yes, slurping is allowed! These are ideally eaten quickly – I mean, that is part of the joy of slurping down somen noodles!

This makes double the mentsuyu sauce needed, because it keeps well in the fridge.

VARIATION: For vegetarians, leave out the katsuobushi flakes or substitute with a dried shiitake mushroom that you've rehydrated first.

SERVES 4

400 g (14 oz) dried somen noodles

MENTSUYU DIPPING SAUCE

60 ml (¼ cup) sake

125 ml (½ cup) mirin

125 ml (½ cup) soy sauce

5 cm (2 in) square piece of kombu

10 g (1 packed cup) katsuobushi flakes

GARNISHES

freshly grated knob of ginger

dab of wasabi

2 spring onions (scallions) or handful of chives, finely chopped

2 teaspoons toasted sesame seeds

katsuobushi flakes

shredded shiso leaves

fine strips of nori

Put the mentsuyu sauce ingredients in a saucepan, bring to a gentle simmer and cook for 5 minutes. Strain to remove the kombu and katsuobushi, pressing out all the sauce. This will keep in the fridge for a month in this concentrated form, but needs to be diluted (one part sauce to three parts water) before use. Only dilute what you need at the time.

When ready to eat, pour 125 ml (½ cup) concentrated mentsuyu into a jug and add 375 ml (1½ cups) water (hot or cold is up to you – with somen noodles I like it cold). Stir well and pour into 4 small bowls for serving. Arrange the garnishes in small bowls, too.

Cook the noodles in boiling water according to the packet directions (they are so thin, they usually cook in 2 minutes). Drain and rinse in cold water. Keep in iced water until ready to eat – they won't stick to each other while in iced water. When ready to serve, divide the noodles onto plates and enjoy immediately.

The noodles will clump together as they cool, so you could serve slow-eaters their noodles in individual bowls of iced water. Then they just need to take care to let the water drip off their noodles before dipping, so they don't water down the dipping sauce too much.

マグロのたたき

TUNA TATAKI WITH PONZU SAUCE

MAGURO NO TATAKI

This classic and elegant dish, with its special combination of lightly seared tuna and aromatic ponzu sauce, is quick and easy to make at home.

We don't eat tuna frequently, but when we do I look for certified sustainable tuna. Fresh yellowfin tuna would be the best choice for most people in the world, except if it is from the Indian Ocean, where stocks are not great. Bluefin is not sustainable, except from MSC-certified fisheries in Japan. You can also use other fish for this, of course: kingfish or sea bream fillets would be wonderful.

Yuzu may not be easy to obtain fresh outside Japan – neither is it the juiciest of citrus, so you would need quite a few. But you can buy bottled yuzu juice and I highly recommend seeking it out, as the unique perfume of yuzu is what makes ponzu so special. If you cannot get yuzu, try mixing together lemon and orange, or Meyer lemon, or even grapefruit – yuzu is a bit sweeter than regular lemon, which would be too sharp. You can also double this amount and save the sauce in a jar in the fridge: it keeps well for a couple of weeks and you can use it as a dressing for salads, tofu and noodles.

VARIATION: Vegans, try this with chilled, sliced firm tofu. The combination of daikon and ponzu sauce on tofu is one of my favourites.

SERVES 4 as a starter

300 g (10½ oz) fresh tuna fillet
generous pinch of salt
5 cm (2 in) piece of daikon, grated
1 spring onion (scallion), finely chopped
pinch of sesame seeds

PONZU SAUCE
2 tablespoons yuzu juice
2 tablespoons soy sauce
1 tablespoon mirin
1.5 cm (about ½ in) piece of kombu

For the ponzu sauce, put the yuzu juice, soy sauce and mirin in a small pan, bring to the boil, then turn off the heat, add the kombu and let it infuse overnight. Remove the kombu and your ponzu sauce is ready. This will keep in the fridge in a jar for up to 2 weeks.

Season the tuna all over with salt. Heat a heavy, non-stick pan (I like cast-iron) over medium–high heat. Sear the tuna for about 10 seconds on each side, depending on its thickness – leave it a little longer if it's particularly thick. Let it rest for a couple of minutes before slicing.

Slice the tuna on an angle, about 5 mm (¼ in) thick, and arrange on a plate. Squeeze the grated daikon to remove the excess liquid and arrange over the middle of the tuna slices. Sprinkle with spring onion and sesame seeds.

Pour a couple of tablespoons of ponzu sauce over the top – over the daikon, in particular, so it spreads into the sauce. Enjoy immediately.

いわしの蒲焼き

KABAYAKI SARDINES

IWASHI NO KABAYAKI

I adore unagi (grilled eel); it's always been a very special treat in my family. My obaachan would order lacquered boxes of unagi layered on rice from her favourite unagi shop to eat at home. My uncle likes to take us to dinner at his favourite unagi restaurant, where, to take in the action, you sit at the counter and watch the preparation of the live eels – the chef first drives a nail through the head directly on his chopping board, then deftly fillets and skewers them for grilling over coals.

Unagi isn't something you would normally make at home: it is always a restaurant delicacy, not only for the preparation of the slippery live eels, but also for the smoky charcoal grills. However, this version with sardines is so quick and easy to make at home – not to mention sustainable, unlike eel – and it replicates the flavour and texture I so love.

If you can get butterflied sardines, this is an incredibly quick meal to make – the cooking is all but 5 minutes. You could also fry the sardines or even cook them on a barbecue, but I find grilling them easiest. Just be careful not to overcook them as this is so quick.

VARIATION: For vegans, use fried or roasted eggplant (aubergine) slices instead of sardines.

SERVES 3–4

12 plump sardines, butterflied
potato starch (or katakuriko starch)
steamed rice (page 36), to serve
pinch of sansho pepper

KABAYAKI SAUCE
2 tablespoons soy sauce
2 tablespoons mirin
2 tablespoons sake
2 tablespoons sugar

To butterfly sardines yourself, scale and remove the heads first. Use your hands rather than a knife: this is called 'tebiraki'. Remove the guts (make an incision with a knife along the belly first) and then, because a sardine is so tender, you can run your thumb and thumbnail along the length of the body to open it up like a book. Use your thumbnail again to separate the bones, and especially the spine, from the flesh. Cut the spine from the tail, and I like to snip off the fin that runs along the backbone with a pair of scissors too.

To make the kabayaki sauce, put all the ingredients in a small saucepan and simmer over medium heat for 2–3 minutes. Don't take your eye off it – the sugar in this small amount of liquid can burn easily if the heat is too high. You want to reduce it ever so slightly.

Preheat your grill or oven to its hottest setting. Dust the sardines in potato starch – this helps keep them moist and the crust soaks up the sauce nicely.

Arrange the sardines on a grill pan or baking tray and place under the hot grill (or on the highest oven shelf) for 2 minutes. Remove and baste with kabayaki sauce, using a pastry brush, then grill for another 2–3 minutes, depending on the size of your sardines. Baste again.

To serve, place the sardines on top of large bowls of rice and baste again so that the kabayaki sauce seeps into the rice and flavours it too. Finish with a sprinkle of sansho pepper.

つくね

CHICKEN MEATBALLS

TSUKUNE

You can often order tsukune in a yakitori shop, along with a variety of other chicken cuts grilled on sticks over coals. It might come as one long patty or smaller balls piled onto the stick; or, sometimes, without even the sticks and as flatter patties. In some places the ground chicken might have crunchy cartilage through it (chicken cartilage is a valuable food in Japan, both for its texture and its richness in collagen). But at home it's much easier to make these as regular meatballs, simply pan-fried and then finished in a characteristic teriyaki sauce.

These are great on their own as an appetiser, or turn them into the main meal with rice, miso soup and some pickles. They're also perfect in bento boxes or added to a donburi.

VARIATIONS: Use any white fish instead of chicken – because the fish is softer, it will make flatter patties. For a vegan version, use fork-mashed tofu (but not silken tofu, which is too moist). This is basically a tofu fritter known as ganmodoki, and it usually has finely chopped onion, carrot and hijiki added, which gives it a colourful, speckled appearance.

SERVES 3–4 as a starter

300 g (10½ oz) boneless chicken thighs or chicken mince
4 cm (1½ in) piece of ginger, grated
¼ teaspoon salt
1 egg white
3–4 tablespoons potato starch
1 tablespoon vegetable oil
shichimi togarashi (optional)
mayonnaise (optional)

TERIYAKI SAUCE
2 tablespoons mirin
2 tablespoons sake
3 tablespoons soy sauce
1 tablespoon sugar (or honey)

If you're using chicken thighs, mince them in a food processor, including any skin or fat – they make for juicier meatballs. Add the ginger, salt, egg white and potato starch and pulse to fully combine. If you're using mince, mix it all together in a bowl until well combined and a bit sticky.

With wet hands, roll the mixture into 12 balls and slightly flatten.

Mix the teriyaki sauce ingredients in a bowl.

Heat the vegetable oil in a non-stick pan over medium–high heat. Fry the meatballs for about 2 minutes on each side until golden brown.

Reduce the heat to medium and add the sauce to the pan, allowing it to sizzle for a moment. Flip the meatballs so the sauce coats them on all sides – do this quickly so the soy sauce doesn't burn.

Serve immediately, perhaps with a sprinkle of shichimi togarashi and some mayonnaise.

醤油プリン

SOY SAUCE PUDDING

SHOYU PURIN

There is a history of soy sauce-making on Shodo Island in the Seto Inland Sea in southern Japan. It is there you will find one of the most wonderful artisanal soy sauce makers: Yamaroku. We tasted this pudding several times during our stay on the island. The soy sauce adds a subtly salty, almost nutty flavour to this beloved classic, in the same way that salt works wonders when added to caramel or chocolate. I am absolutely hooked on it.

The recipe is very similar to creme caramel, or what the Italians call 'latte alla portoghese', but Japanese 'purin' has a subtle difference: it is simply made with milk and whole eggs. There is no cream here, and no extra egg yolks as in latte alla portoghese. To me, it is a little less rich and has a lighter mouth-feel. It is very, very easy to eat.

If you have a special soy sauce, such as a barrel-aged or twice-fermented, now would be a good time to experiment with it.

SERVES 6

500 ml (2 cups) full-cream milk
50 g (¼ cup) sugar
3 teaspoons soy sauce
4 eggs

CARAMEL
65 g (⅓ cup) sugar

Preheat the oven to 160°C (320°F). Arrange 6 ramekins in a deep baking dish.

To make the caramel, put the sugar in a small pan with 1 tablespoon water. Place over low heat and watch the sugar carefully as it begins to melt, then simmer and, finally, turn amber. Resist the urge to stir but just let it do its thing, at least until the very end, when a swirl of the pan can help. When it begins to colour, it will do so very quickly so be ready to remove it from the heat at deep amber – too dark and it will be bitter. I don't need to tell you that hot caramel is incredibly dangerous, so don't let a drop touch your skin!

Immediately pour the hot caramel into the ramekins (a spoon can be useful, or pour freehand). It solidifies very quickly, so don't worry if it doesn't cover the bottom of the ramekin – it will all come out perfectly in the end. Set aside.

Warm the milk and sugar in a saucepan over medium heat. As soon as you can see bubbles around the edge and the milk is steaming, take it off the heat before it can simmer. Add the soy sauce and have a taste – if you would like a stronger soy sauce flavour, add another teaspoon. Leave to cool slightly.

Whisk the eggs gently by hand in a bowl – a machine will make them too frothy and you'll have puddings filled with holes. Once the milk has cooled to warm bath temperature, add it to the eggs. Pour into the ramekins.

Fill the baking dish with hot water and put in the oven (if it's a heavy dish, it's safer to put it in the oven, then add water).

Bake for 25 minutes or until the custard has set – it will be wobbly to the touch but the top will be lightly browned.

Cool completely before serving, or they can be chilled until needed. They will keep in the fridge for 3 days.

To serve, run a knife around the edge of the ramekin and hold a plate over the top (ideally one with a bit of a lip to catch the caramel), then flip everything over in one swift movement so the pudding turns out.

みたらし団子

RICE BALLS WITH SWEET SOY SAUCE

MITARASHI DANGO

When I was little, I didn't appreciate the sweet–soy flavour of mitarashi sauce on dango sticks. Was it meant to be a sweet sauce? Was it meant to be savoury? It was too much of both and my ultimate dango were those smothered in anko – the sweet red bean paste that is still one of my favourite things in the world (page 256).

But, as I've grown older, I appreciate the not-too-sweet, almost nutty, mitarashi topping on this quintessential snack. In fact, it has become a flavour that hits me with nostalgia whenever I taste it – now, when I'm given the choice of anko or mitarashi dango, I choose the latter.

Dango are made with shiratamako flour, making them slightly different from mochi, which are made with pounded rice. These are largely inspired by Maori Murota's dango from her cookbook, one of my favourites, *Tokyo Cult Recipes*. They are made with silken tofu mixed into the dough and are so wonderfully light and chewy I have to stop myself eating them before I've even made the mitarashi sauce.

You need a bowl of iced water at the ready when making these, and at least three wooden skewers. And it might be difficult to find shiratamako flour outside Japan; it's a clumpy, glutinous rice flour for making mochi – if you can't find it, use mochiko flour.

MAKES 3 skewers

75 g (2¾ oz) silken tofu
60 g (½ cup) shiratamako flour

MITARASHI SAUCE

1 tablespoon brown sugar
2 tablespoons soy sauce
2 teaspoons kuzu starch (or potato starch)

Stir the silken tofu and flour together to make a lovely smooth dough. Roll it into a log and cut into 9 pieces. Roll each piece into a ball.

Bring a pot of water to the boil, add the dango and cook for about 2 minutes, or until they float. Lift out and plunge into iced water to cool. Drain and thread onto skewers, 3 dango to each skewer. These are often charred in a wire grill basket to give a good toasty flavour – cooking in a cast-iron pan will give you the same nice char.

For the mitarashi sauce, stir the sugar, soy sauce and starch in a small saucepan with 60 ml (¼ cup) water until smooth. Cook over low–medium heat, stirring, for a couple of minutes until thickened. Spoon over the grilled dango.

You can make both the dango and sauce a few hours in advance, keep separate and heat up when ready to serve, but dango are best eaten the day they're made.

かりんとう

KARINTO

These traditional crisp fried snacks have a mysterious past. Some believe Karinto date back to the Nara period (the eighth century) as a sweet treat reserved for the elite; others think they were introduced from abroad, either by the Chinese, or in the 16th century by the Portuguese, who brought other fried dishes such as tempura. Either way, Karinto were a beloved street food by the 1800s. You can now even find savoury versions, with flavours of Japanese curry, sesame or even wasabi, but the most traditional are these deep, dark caramel ones.

Karinto are not something you would usually make at home, partly because, if you live in Japan, there are many wonderful speciality shops selling them. But, since I don't, I was delighted to find out how easy they are to make. My friend, Yuta Mizoguchi, a wonderful chef, showed me how to roll and fry these and, up to that stage, they reminded me of Tuscan 'cenci', a special fried carnival treat dusted in powdered sugar. But then the fried pieces of dough went into a dark caramel sauce, traditionally made with black sugar from Okinawa, which imparts an almost balsamic flavour and creates a hard coating. I put a splash of soy sauce in the caramel, which gives it a salty edge. Use the full 2 teaspoons of soy sauce if you want a more pronounced flavour, and 1 teaspoon for a subtle hint – I prefer the former. These are wonderful with a cup of green tea, or even sake.

MAKES 50–60

100 g (⅔ cup) plain (all-purpose) flour
½ teaspoon baking powder
2 teaspoons sugar
2 teaspoons vegetable oil
pinch of salt
60 ml (¼ cup) water (or as needed)
vegetable oil, for frying

CARAMEL

120 g (4½ oz) black Okinawan sugar (or brown sugar)
1 teaspoon water
1–2 teaspoons soy sauce

Combine the flour, baking powder, sugar, oil and salt in a bowl and mix until you have a shaggy dough. Transfer to a lightly floured surface and knead to a springy, smooth dough. Let this rest for at least 10 minutes, covered.

Roll the dough into a long oval about 3–5 mm (¼ in) thick. Cut into long strips, about 5 cm (2 in) wide, and then into 5 mm (¼ in) sticks.

Pour vegetable oil into a small saucepan to about 3 cm (1 inch) deep. Heat to 160°C (320°F) over medium heat. When it's hot enough that a chopstick inserted into the oil is immediately surrounded by lots of tiny bubbles, start frying the dough sticks – you might need to do this in batches. Fry for about 2 minutes until golden brown. Remove and drain on kitchen paper.

While the dough sticks are cooling, heat the caramel ingredients in a saucepan over low heat until the sugar has dissolved. Simmer gently until you can draw a line on the bottom of the pan with a wooden spoon. Remove from the heat and toss the karinto immediately into the hot caramel until coated – you might also need to do this in a couple of batches. Let them dry on a wire cooling rack. They should turn matte and not be sticky once completely cooled.

These keep well in an airtight container for several days.

味噌

MISO

味噌

MISO

'Everything is all right as long as there is miso.'

JAPANESE PROVERB

This thick fermented paste, made of soybeans and rice or barley, is one of the most beloved Japanese ingredients, both inside and outside the country. Tracing miso's history gives an extremely interesting glimpse into Japanese culture in general.

The precise origins of miso are not clear, but most historians agree the idea of miso arrived from China, either directly or via Korea, sometime in the sixth or seventh century, initially as a food reserved only for temples and nobles. In this scenario, then, miso shares an ancestor with soy sauce, which was introduced to Japan from China in the seventh century by Buddhist monks. Both miso and soy sauce are based on the same ingredients, after all – soybeans, grains and salt, plus, of course, koji culture to ferment it all.

This fermented soybean-based condiment had already had a very long history in China, initially as a fermented fish condiment that William Shurtleff and Akiko Aoyagi, the authors of *History of Miso and Soybean Chiang*, say: '… laid the foundation for the later development of miso, and enabled people long ago to break the vicious cycle of feast and famine, conserving foods from times of bounty to be enjoyed in times of scarcity.'

Chinese doujiang (chunky soybean paste, also known today as doubanjiang 豆瓣醬) and Korean doenjang are also related to this condiment, and their histories are interwoven as well. You can tell this from the etymology, starting with the Chinese word 'jiang': paste. The Chinese for soy sauce, jiangyou, means 'liquid pressed from jiang', implying that jiang is a preparation that is older than soy sauce (in fact, historians consider it likely to be 1000 years older). When Chinese characters arrived in Japan, jiang (醬) was also used by the Japanese to describe soybean paste and in seventh century Japan this character was pronounced 'hishio'. Just a few decades later, it was also pronounced 'misho'. You can see where this is going.

The *Chou-li* (*Rituals of the Chou Dynasty*) from the royal Chinese court from the sixth to eighth century BC contains one of the earliest references to jiang, describing it as 'made by mixing the meat of animals, birds, and fish with millet, koji and salt, then pickling it in wine in a crock for a hundred days'. It already sounds like miso, but the first mention of soybeans used in jiang in place of animal products dates to the first century BC. This early seasoning had a consistency that was like a mix between miso and soy sauce; not firm, but not liquid.

There was also, however, another very early Japanese condiment that developed separately from miso and dates to the neolithic Jomon period. This fermented condiment was made from sea salt and seafood such as shellfish, squid, bonito, eels and sardines (and, quite often, just the intestines were used – not dissimilar to Ancient Roman 'garum') and kept in pickling crocks. Examples of these crocks from 3000–4000 years ago were found in the north-eastern regions, still known as the central miso-producing area of Japan. Shurtleff and Aoyagi note: 'Today, the northeastern provinces are known as the "miso heartland" of Japan; the per-capita consumption there is the highest in the nation and the ancient homemade-miso tradition is still very much alive. These facts, combined with the archaeological evidence indicating early mastery of salt-pickling and fermentation, move some scholars to go so far as to trace the origins of miso (and shoyu) to this part of Japan rather than to China or Korea.'

Whichever way it began, in its early days miso was so precious that it was considered a form of currency. In the Heian period (794–1185) it was a luxury made with expensive polished rice and available only to the nobility. It wasn't yet used as a condiment, but was seen as a food in its own right – spread onto other foods or even licked.

The kanji for miso changed around this time, from hishio (borrowing the Chinese jiang 醤) to today's 味噌, which is a combination of mi, meaning 'flavour' and so, 'throat'. Shurtleff and Aoyagi suggest that this important change meant miso was now being considered a Japanese food, rather than a borrowed Chinese import, and deserved its own Japanese word.

During the Kamakura period (1185–1333), another important step occurred in the timeline: miso soup developed and spread throughout Japan, thanks to the important influence of Buddhism in daily life. Zen Buddhist temples not only served their shojin cuisine to common people, but almost all of them made their own miso and taught others how to as well.

The typical Buddhist meal – a large serving of grains, with pickles and miso soup of tofu and vegetables – became part of the standard Japanese diet. Miso soup, which has always been a uniquely Japanese dish, was also a favourite pick for samurai warriors on the battlefield – miso paste is a rich source of protein and easily transportable.

Miso, in fact, became recognised by all Japanese, rich and poor, as an important life-saving food in times of famine, hence the proverb, *miso sae areba*: 'everything is all right as long as there is miso'.

In the Muromachi period (1336–1573) Japanese farmers began not only to grow their own soybeans but also produce their own miso, often using 'poorer' grains, such as millet and barley, in place of rice. Shurtleff and Aoyagi recount that this was partly thanks to the important daimyo Takeda Shingen (1521–1573), who encouraged farmers to grow soybeans and make miso so that his samurai could have a good supply wherever they went.

Two things happened during this period, not uncoincidentally: miso became an everyday staple and the miso that we know today took form. Hatcho miso and white miso both date to this time. You can also find references to miso in stories, music and performance arts of the era, displaying what an important part of the culture this food had become.

The year that Takeda Shingen died, Francesco Carletti was born into an Italian merchant family in Florence. He became the first private voyager to circumnavigate the world – just him and his father, Antonio, without a fleet, but under the protection of Ferdinando I de' Medici. The young Florentine spent nine months in Japan from June 1597 to March 1598. His account, *Ragionamenti di Francesco Carletti Fiorentino*, published posthumously in 1701, is fascinating as one of the first western descriptions of Japanese secular life.

Carletti spends a lot of time on food (what else would we expect from a Florentine?), including the first western description of miso and how it is made. I have translated these from 16th-century Italian. (Note, the original text calls miso 'Misol' and what Carletti calls 'sciro' would be pronounced 'shiro'; I believe he means shiru, 汁, or soup. I would also point out that he uses the word 'piccante' to describe the miso, which does not necessarily mean 'spicy', as it does today, but can mean simply pungent or flavourful.)

'They have certain large, bloody fish that they use for this dish [sashimi] ... and others, which they flavour with a certain sauce that they call Misol [sic], made with a sort of bean that is in abundance, that is cooked and mashed and mixed with some rice and then left alone, packed into a tub and, all but decaying, it becomes stronger of flavour, like Formento [frumento: wheat] but more acute and pungent, which, using a little at a time, gives flavour to their dishes, that they call Sciro [shiro, or shiru] and we would call Intingolo [a sauce or potage].'

Carletti goes on to describe in great detail how chopsticks are used, the tableware of red-lacquered bowls, how sake is made and served, and his difficulty in finding red meat. It's an entertaining read – he lists the birds he ate to satisfy his craving for meat in pescatarian Japan, and his thoughts as a Tuscan on how well one could live in Japan, especially if they were to plant some olives (olives would grow well, he noted) and vineyards.

However, it wasn't until the second half of the 1800s that Europeans would taste miso again. Just five years after Carletti's visit, Japan began to turn inward and, fearing colonialism, it closed itself off from the world. By 1635 trade was restricted and the shogun issued a decree that no Japanese were allowed out of the country. This was the Edo period, and the country's borders remained closed for some 265 years until the mid-1800s, when America essentially forced them to open for trade.

During this time of fierce isolationism, but also of peace and stability, many Japanese ingredients were developed, refined and perfected: sake, soy sauce, vinegar, mirin, dashi, as well as miso. Miso's popularity as an everyday staple surged; there was so much demand for miso in Edo (the ancient name for Tokyo) that farmers could not keep up with production. As people flocked to the city of Edo, miso shops flourished, as did restaurants offering miso soup and other miso-based dishes.

When Japan re-opened to the world in 1868, it had missed almost three centuries of scientific and technological advancement. The new Emperor appointed top European professors and scientists to take high positions at Tokyo's university and many enthusiastically took to studying koji and miso, which they had never before experienced. Microscopes only reached Japan in the 1880s – for the first time Japanese scientists and miso producers could fully understand the microbiology behind their favourite food.

During the Second World War there was a dramatic shift in the standardisation of food production, with sudden strict government controls. For miso, this meant controls over the types and grades that could be produced and, as a result, many rare varieties disappeared. The food shortages during and after the war also made miso production more industrialised and it went into decline.

Eventually, miso made a comeback and – just like the cheese- and wine-makers of Europe – artisan producers went back to traditional ways of making miso in kioke barrels. This was partly fuelled by interest in its health benefits – miso is nutrient dense, probiotic and a complete protein, especially when consumed with rice. It is known to boost digestion and the immune system, and there are many studies reporting that miso consumption, especially of long-fermented miso, reduces the risk of cancer.

TYPES OF MISO

Today there are no clear criteria for miso – unlike the Japanese Agricultural Standards for soy sauce – which makes it hard to categorise. There are currently more than 1000 producers and an equal number of types of miso, including a huge range of regional varieties.

All miso is made from boiled or steamed soybeans, koji and salt. The type of koji used (koji grown on rice, on barley or on soybeans) and how long it's fermented, gives a variety of results that can affect colour, flavour, quality and texture.

Kome miso is made with rice koji and is the most common miso, making up about 80 per cent of the miso types you will find in Japan.

Mugi miso comes from the south and is made with barley koji, which gives it a sweet, deep flavour. **Mame miso** is made in central Japan with whole, rather than mashed, soybeans. Mugi and mame make up five per cent each. The remaining ten per cent is **awase miso** – blended miso.

Hatcho miso comes from Aichi prefecture in central Japan and is classified as mame miso. It is made using only soybeans and salt – no grains. This interesting miso is deep, dark and strongly flavoured, because it is usually fermented for two to three years.

You will also see miso categorised by colour...

Shiro miso (white miso) is sweeter, the least salty and most delicately flavoured, as it is fermented for less time. It has a higher ratio of koji, which contributes to its sweetness.

Aka miso (red miso) is made with a greater proportion of soybeans and longer fermenting, for a more robust flavour and darker colour. This is the one to use for heartier dishes – winter stews and marinades, for example.

In between, you have yellow miso, **tanshoku miso**. This is the most versatile of the three miso colour types and will have characteristics of both white and red. You can – and should – blend miso yourself, combining two or three different types to make a custom miso.

You can also find flavoured misos, such as **yuzu miso**, which can be used as a dressing or marinade, or added to a soup stock.

There are many wonderful kinds of miso that are named after their local area. To pick out just a few:

Sendai miso from the north is a traditional, long-fermented variety that has been handed down from samurai.

Saikyo miso from Kyoto is the sweet, delicate miso that is preferred for New Year's soup in the Kansai region.

Hokkaido miso from the far north is delicate and goes well with locally caught salmon.

Setouchi miso, from the area around the Seto Inland Sea, is made of barley miso and has a light, fragrant, sweet style.

HOW TO STORE MISO

Store-bought Japanese miso is often sold in its own handy little box, or a bag. It is shelf stable at room temperature until it is opened and then you should keep it in the fridge. It will keep for a very long time – years – if stored properly. That also goes for homemade miso. Depending on your climate, it can be stored in a cool, dark pantry while it is fermenting and aging, and even when you start using it. In very warm weather, I recommend keeping it in the fridge once it is ready to use.

手づくり味噌

HOMEMADE MISO

TEZUKURI MISO

For the longest time I thought that making miso at home would be a daunting task. Then, several years ago, I finally took an online class with Yuki Gomi, who teaches Japanese cooking from her London home. She helped me realise not only how easy and fun it is (get the whole family involved!), but that having my own stash of delicious miso to last me for years was the greatest gift. This is also a wonderful way to get into the world of koji (page 8), if you want to learn more about the magic of Japanese ferments.

I took another class in Chino, Nagano, with Junko Ariura in her home, where we sat outside by her kura (the traditional storehouses where crocks of miso and other important treasures were kept secure) and cooked the soybeans and grilled mochi over an open fire and made miso in the late autumn air. She showed me how to make everything by hand, literally. We squeezed the beans together with her homemade rice koji and fistfuls of salt with our hands, rather than blending with a machine. The kids helped, too, with Junko's nodding approval. 'It is very good to have children make miso. They have good bacteria,' she explained. In fact, Junko warned us all not to use hand sanitiser before making miso as it would kill all this good bacteria. Like all fermented things, the natural yeasts and bacteria in the air and on our hands will all add to the biodiversity of the microflora and be a part of the end product. I know this will be a particularly special batch – born in mountainous Nagano and raised in the Tuscan countryside.

This recipe is inspired by both Yuki's and Junko's methods. The recipes are similar, but Yuki uses a little more koji than soybeans and quite a bit more salt than Junko, who favours a more traditional recipe of half and half soybeans to koji, with the salt amount being ten per cent of the weight of the boiled soybeans and koji together (the beans will double, at least, in weight once boiled).

Koji teacher Nakaji-san, makes a sweet miso with twice the usual amount of koji (to show off the koji he makes, naturally). You too can adjust miso to your liking: this is one of the beauties of homemade miso. More koji and less salt makes for a sweeter, more delicate miso; more salt and longer fermentation will create a stronger flavour and colour.

There are very few ingredients here, so let's be selective about them: real, unrefined sea salt; good-quality dried soybeans, organic if you can (if you cannot get soybeans, try this with chickpeas); and rice koji – order it online or learn how to make it yourself. The materials you need are quite simple: a bowl or tray, your hands and time – time is the main ingredient here.

You also need sterilised jars. I would suggest small jars if you want to give some away to friends, have a small fridge or don't use miso very often. This will fill two 1-litre jars, four 500 ml (2 cup) jars, or eight 250 ml (1 cup) jars, or any combination.

To sterilise the jars, wash them and the lids in hot, soapy water, rinse and place upside down on a baking tray and dry them out in a 150°C (300°F) oven for about 10 minutes. If you are using jars with rubbers seal, don't put them in the oven: they need to be sterilised in boiling water and left to dry. I also like Junko's method for sanitising jars – she simply adds a splash of shochu or gin and wipes it out.

MAKES about 2 kg (4 lb 6 oz)

500 g (1 lb 2 oz) dried yellow soybeans
500 g (1 lb 2 oz) rice koji
150 g (5½ oz) sea salt (or as needed)

Ideally, start by soaking the soybeans the night before, for at least 12 hours or overnight – rinse, then soak them in a large bowl of water.

Drain the soybeans, put in a large pot and cover with fresh water. Bring to the boil and simmer, covered, until you can easily squeeze a bean between your thumb and forefinger – this can take 2–4 hours, depending on the beans, but if you have a pressure cooker you can do it in 20–30 minutes.

When the beans are ready, run your hands through the koji to remove any lumps. Add 50 g (1¾ oz) of the salt and mix well.

Drain the beans, keeping about a cupful of cooking water for later. Weigh the beans and calculate 10 per cent of their weight – that is how much salt you will later add. For example, if the beans weigh 1 kg (2 lb 3 oz), add 100 g (3½ oz) of salt.

Place the beans in a large bowl and, when cool enough to touch, start squeezing and mashing them together with your hands. You can also use a potato masher or, if you want a particularly smooth miso, put them in a food processor. However, I feel the act of making miso, as I learned from Junko, really needs your hands, rather than metal blades. Also, I am quite fond of a chunky miso.

Once the beans are cooled to around body temperature (above 60°C could kill the koji), add the koji and the salt you weighed. Mash and mix until everything is very, very well combined. If it seems too dry, add some of the reserved bean water (if you've forgotten to save it, just add warm water) until it has a firm paste consistency. If you add a significant amount of water, add a bit more salt – 10 per cent of the amount of water, as we did with the beans (so, if you add 100 ml/3½ fl oz water, add 10 g/¼ oz of salt).

That's it; the miso is done and ready to pack into jars.

Continued ›

PACKING THE MISO INTO JARS

The traditional way is to throw the balls into the jar to force out any air bubbles (this is obviously easier to do with a large jar or crock). You can also place the balls in the jar and punch them down or push them down firmly with the end of a rolling pin. You simply want to push out all the air pockets.

Leave about 2 cm (¾ in) clear at the top of the jar – this is space for the shoyu to come out (a delicious light-coloured liquid related to tamari). Smooth the top and sprinkle with a layer of salt, in particular around the edges, to help prevent any undesired mould forming.

Place a disc of baking paper or cling film over the top, in direct contact with the miso, and put on the lid. Write the date on the jar and leave it to ferment in a cool, dark place for at least six months but a year is even better.

By cool, I mean it should be indoor autumn/winter temperature, which is the traditional time of the year to make miso, at least for the first month while the fermentation is new. (I once made the mistake of making miso at the start of a Tuscan summer heatwave and ruined a batch.)

After the first month, Nakaji points out, you can keep miso between 15–30°C (60–85°F) without any problems. Do check it now and then to ensure there is no sign of black mould growing – remove it, if you do find any.

Once you have opened the jars, store in the fridge. They will keep perfectly for years; mine were still going strong for two years until I finished them all. In fact, try waiting two or three years for the most delicious results.

JUNKO'S TIPS

If you are impatient and want to eat your homemade miso at six months, flip the miso over and start eating it from the bottom, which will be better fermented. Otherwise, wait for a year. Or even better, two or three. At any rate, at some point in the miso's lifetime you're going to realise, one day, *this is the best it's been!* Now, if you'd like to keep the miso at that flavour profile, refrigerate or even freeze it so that you stop the fermentation and keep it as it is. It's a great reminder that, like any fermented product, miso is alive and will keep changing.

NAKAJI'S TIP

If you have a favourite homemade miso on hand, spread a thin layer of it on top of your new miso. This adds microbes essential for fermentation and will also help prevent bad mould from growing on the surface. If you have it, you can also spread sake lees (preferably from junmai sake, see page 136) on the surface for a similar reason.

味噌漬け

MISO PICKLES

MISOZUKE

These easy pickles pack a punch, thanks to the miso, which does everything here. I think white miso, or a sweeter, more delicate miso is particularly nice for this; a very strong miso can be overpowering.

As with any of the other pickle recipes in this book, you can use a variety of different seasonal vegetables here – I like root vegetables especially for this, such as radishes, carrots, daikon, turnips, but cucumbers also work well. If you have very fresh, just-picked dainty radishes with pretty leaves, they are very nice pickled whole, leaves and all.

Things that might often be wasted, such as radish tops or turnip tops, are great pickled. Also, continuing in the Japanese spirit of no waste or mottainai (page 226), don't throw away the leftover miso – you can use it for another batch of pickles or keep it for soup.

MAKES about 150 g (½ cup)

140 g (about ½ cup) radishes
2 tablespoons white miso

Wash the radishes thoroughly (if you are keeping the leaves, pay careful attention, as dirt at the base of the leaves is very stubborn). I like to keep these whole if they are quite small, but halve them, keeping the leaves intact, if they are larger. Pat them dry.

Coat the radishes entirely in miso – there's no better way to do this than simply with your hands in a bowl. Rub the miso paste all over them, place in an airtight container or resealable bag and leave them to marinate for at least an hour; or, even better, overnight.

Before serving, wipe off the excess miso. These are best eaten straightaway, or the next day. They can be stored in the container or the bag you pickled them in.

ネギ味噌

MISO & GREEN ONION SAUCE

NEGI MISO

This is a delicious sauce for a variety of dishes: use a spoonful to top grilled meat, fish, eggplant (aubergine) or tofu; add to a side dish of steamed broccoli or cooked spinach; try it with rice (a cherry-sized blob inside onigiri, on top of steamed rice or brushed onto rice cakes instead of the miso walnut paste, page 74). Use it to flavour a bowl of ramen or a stir-fry. It's great, too, as a dip for vegetable sticks. I think there's really no end to what you can improve with a bit of negi miso.

The quality and flavour of the miso will make a difference here – try mixing different misos to customise the flavour. If you like heat, add some fresh or dried chilli to this.

Negi is a Japanese green onion that is slightly thicker and longer than a spring onion – almost like a thin leek. In fact, you could try leeks in this recipe, although they would need a little longer cooking to get to the soft and wilted stage.

MAKES about 185 ml (¾ cup)

- 6–8 green tops of spring onions (scallions)
- 1 teaspoon sesame oil
- 1 tablespoon brown sugar
- 60 ml (¼ cup) sake
- 110 g (4 oz) miso

Finely chop the spring onion tops. Put in a saucepan with the sesame oil and cook gently over low heat for 10–15 minutes, or until they are wilted and softened.

Add the sugar and sake to the pan, stirring to dissolve the sugar. Allow the alcohol to cook off and evaporate a little, then turn off the heat and add the miso. Stir to a thick, luscious sauce – it should be more fluid than miso but not runny. If you need to, add a splash of water.

This keeps very well in a jar in the fridge for a month.

味噌汁

MISO SOUP

Miso soup has been an important feature of all Japanese meals, especially breakfast, for centuries. During the Kamakura period (1185–1333), Buddhist temple cuisine introduced the idea of a perfectly balanced meal, known as *ichiju-sansai* – 'one soup, three dishes'. It is still considered a non-negotiable part of any meal and is one of the fixtures of home cooking – the aroma of a pot of warm miso soup teleports me straight to my grandmother's dining room. It is something you will find in all parts of Japan, served at Japanese restaurants of all levels, offered at hotel breakfasts and traditional inns, even in convenience stores and fast-food restaurants. There are, of course, instant packet versions, where you only need add hot water. But nothing compares to a bowl of homemade miso.

There are infinite versions of miso soup because you can continually change the ingredients and that is why Japanese people never tire of it. You can use seasonal vegetables, such as spinach, pumpkin, carrot, leek, chunks of eggplant (aubergine) or cabbage. Or pull out dried pantry items, such as shiitake mushrooms or wakame seaweed.

There isn't usually meat in miso soup (tonjiru, page 72, is one exception, and it is heartier) but there are sometimes clams. You will especially find tofu – of all different textures and styles: fried, fresh, freeze-dried, skins – which hints at miso soup's temple origins. Don't just pile things into this though – pick just two, at most three, ingredients.

For the miso, use awase miso, or a mixed/yellow miso that is neither too delicate nor too strong. My mother likes to custom mix her own flavour, using a few different kinds.

SERVES 4

5 cm (2 in) piece of daikon, peeled (or potato)
500 ml (2 cups) dashi (pages 108–9)
handful of baby spinach
dried wakame or diced tofu (optional)
3–4 tablespoons miso
finely chopped spring onion (scallion) (optional)

Slice the daikon into thin rounds, and then halve or quarter, if large. Place in a saucepan with the dashi and bring to a gentle simmer. Cook for 8–10 minutes until tender.

Add the baby spinach – the reason I use this is that it barely needs cooking so you can turn off the heat immediately. If you're adding wakame or tofu, they can go in just before the baby spinach: they only need to warm through.

Now, heat off, add the miso. Since miso paste is so thick, you need to loosen it first. There is a special tool called a misokoshi, essentially a small but deep strainer, for this specific task. But you can use a tea strainer or a ladle – dipping it in the dashi to collect some liquid and then stirring in the miso until you have a sort of slurry, then adding to the dashi. If using a fairly chunky miso, the strainer will capture the rice or barley residue, but personally I like finding these bits at the bottom of a homemade miso soup.

Have a taste: if it is too strong, add water or dashi; if too shy, add a bit more miso. Serve in small bowls. If you want to add spring onions, sprinkle them on just before serving.

豚汁

PORK & VEGETABLE MISO SOUP

TONJIRU

This variation of miso soup is much heartier than the one you usually find accompanying breakfast with rice and pickles and other little dishes. This could even be considered a one-pot meal and it's absolutely perfect on a cold day. The combination of so many vegetables with the pork belly adds a delicious richness. You can vary the vegetables according to the season: napa cabbage, sweet potato, gobo (burdock root: not easy to find outside Japan), onion and leek are great additions. You can also use fresh tofu, diced, in place of the pork.

If you're not familiar with konnyaku or konjac, it is a dark grey jelly (dark because it contains hijiki seaweed) made from the bulb of a subtropical plant, *Amorphophallus konjac*. (It has a number of unappealing names in English: devil's tongue, voodoo lily, snake palm, for example.) Here it adds texture and bulk to the soup. It's vegan and gluten free and is a very popular food in Japan, considered medicinal as it is high in fibre and very good for digestion (there is a reason it is paired with this pork belly). You can also find it in noodle form, known as shirataki; if you can't find dark konnyaku, try these, they are easily found in Asian grocery stores (I can even find them in my local supermarket here in the Tuscan countryside).

The pork belly is sliced paper thin, which means it cooks in no time – it is very easy to buy it like this in Japan. If you have to slice it yourself, place the pork in the freezer for 30 minutes first, so it is firmer and easier to cut.

VARIATION: Vegetarians can leave out the pork or add in one of the suggestions above.

SERVES 4–6

2 dried shiitake mushrooms

3 cm (1½ in) piece of daikon, peeled

½ carrot, peeled

1 medium potato, peeled

2 spring onions (scallions)

100 g (3½ oz) fresh pork belly, thinly sliced

1 litre (4 cups) dashi (pages 108–9)

100 g (3½ oz) konnyaku or firm tofu

2 tablespoons white miso

1 tablespoon soy sauce

Rehydrate the shiitake mushrooms in a little just-boiled water. Drain (save the water to add to the soup) and slice.

Slice the daikon into rounds, then cut into quarters. Slice the carrot and potato similarly. Consider the thickness and size of the root vegetables, so that they cook in a similar time. Cut the white parts of the spring onions into 2–3 cm (1 in) pieces and finely chop the green parts. Set the vegetables aside.

Sear the pork belly in a large pot over medium–high heat. There should be enough fat in the pork to prevent it sticking, but don't worry too much if it does. Cook for a few minutes to brown slightly on both sides.

Add the daikon, carrot and potato to the pot and toss with the pork. Pour in the dashi. Bring the soup to a gentle simmer, covered, and simmer for 5 minutes.

Meanwhile, blanche the konnyaku – this removes some of its seaweed odour – then cut or tear it into small pieces. If you're not using konnyaku, you can replace it with firm tofu, which only needs to be diced.

Add the konnyaku (or tofu) and the white part of the spring onions to the pot of soup and simmer for a further 5 minutes or until the root vegetables feel just tender.

Take off the heat and add the miso, loosening it first. You can do this in a ladle, dipping it into the soup to collect liquid and then stirring in the miso until you have a sort of slurry. Stir back into the soup along with the soy sauce.

Serve immediately, scattered with spring onion tops.

五平餅

RICE CAKES WITH WALNUT MISO

GOHEIMOCHI

Outside Japan, mochi seems to be synonymous with a sweet rice cake made of a very chewy and thin steamed rice-flour dough. I am a fan of these, too, but mochi really just means 'rice cake' and can take many forms, including this one: cakes made with sticky rice lightly pounded by hand.

This special kind of mochi is from the mountains of central Japan, around Nagano, Gifu and Aichi prefectures and dates back to the Edo period (1603–1868). It was a popular portable lunch for people who worked in the forests (gohei sounds like 'gobei', which is a lumberjack), easily heated up by grilling over a fire. The tradition is to enjoy these after the rice harvest in autumn, with guests and the family gathered around.

Sometimes the sauce is a sweet soy sauce mixture, sometimes a sweet and salty miso sauce. I adore the version with walnuts, well grilled over an open fire, which is how I ate these in Nagano, while making miso with Junko-san. Both the rice mochi, squeezed around bamboo sticks for easy handling, and the sauce are grilled over charcoal stoves, which you can replicate with a barbecue. If you don't have an open fire, set these under a hot grill or on the top shelf of a hot oven. The rice toasts quickly and brings out the nutty flavours of the walnut miso on top.

This recipe will leave you with a little extra walnut miso – it is so delicious, you may want to make more. You can use it similarly to negi miso (page 68).

MAKES 6

140 g (5 oz) Japanese rice
250 ml (1 cup) water

WALNUT MISO

60 g (½ cup) shelled walnut pieces
2 tablespoons miso
2 tablespoons brown sugar or honey
½ teaspoon sesame seeds

Put the rice in a sieve and wash a few times to remove the excess starch. Drain and tip into a saucepan. Add the water and bring to a simmer. Cover, reduce the heat to the lowest setting and simmer for 15–17 minutes until the rice is tender. Keep covered and leave to steam off the heat for a further 10 minutes. You can also use a rice cooker for this.

Lightly pound the rice a few times using a suribachi or mortar and pestle (or get creative if you don't have one – the end of a rolling pin and a bowl, for example). It should be a sort of sticky mass but with still visible rice grains.

With wet hands, roll the rice into 6 balls, then push bamboo skewers or popsicle sticks into the balls and shape into flattened ovals around the sticks (they are meant to look like waraji sandals).

To make the walnut miso, grind the walnuts – a suribachi does this perfectly, or use a mortar and pestle. Make this as chunky or smooth as you like. Add the miso and brown sugar and about 1 tablespoon water to loosen the mixture so it is easily spreadable. Taste: it should be delicious but you can adjust the sweetness (sugar) and saltiness (water or miso).

Grill both sides of the rice cakes until nicely toasted. Spread with a layer of walnut miso, sprinkle with sesame seeds and serve immediately.

おやき

FRIED DUMPLINGS WITH MISO EGGPLANT

OYAKI

Oyaki, delicious pan-fried dumplings, come from the volcanic mountainous region of Nagano. With its harsh winters, historically this was not a place where rice was easily grown, so farmers instead cultivated wheat and buckwheat for soba.

As a rather rustic and economical snack, these dumplings are typically filled with vegetables – often mashed pumpkin seasoned with sugar and soy sauce; or miso eggplant (I can highly recommend leftover mabo eggplant, page 85, as a delicious filling, which is what is pictured here); or even pickled turnip greens known as nozawana (page 27). These pickles are not only traditional in Nagano, they're a staple. You can even fill them with something sweet such as anko (red bean paste, page 256). These last two are perhaps the most popular fillings.

You can make this just with regular flour if you don't have buckwheat, but I love the nice nutty flavour and appealing darker colour the buckwheat flour gives to the dough.

I followed Japanese recipe writer Ayako Kidokoro's method for forming and shaping this dough, which is surprisingly easy and very forgiving. (No fancy pleats: just pinch, flatten and cook seam-side-down on the pan to seal it.)

These are best eaten piping hot, but the good news is that they reheat really well, so you can easily make a double batch and have some to reheat later.

MAKES 6 dumplings

- 120 g (about 1 cup) plain (all-purpose) flour
- 2 tablespoons buckwheat flour
- pinch of salt
- 1 teaspoon vegetable oil, plus extra for frying
- 125 ml (½ cup) just-boiled water

FILLING

- 1 tablespoon vegetable oil
- 1 eggplant (aubergine), diced
- 1 tablespoon negi miso (page 68) or regular miso

Combine the flours, salt and 1 teaspoon oil, then pour over the hot water a little at a time as you mix (usually with chopsticks, but a fork is fine too) until you have a shaggy dough. You may not need all the water. You should be able to squeeze the dough and feel it coming together easily without being too sticky. Knead for a few minutes, until smooth, then cover and leave to rest for at least 30 minutes, or up to a day.

For the filling, heat the oil in a frying pan and fry the eggplant, tossing frequently, for about 7 minutes until golden brown on all sides and a fork slips in easily. Add the miso, along with a splash of water to help dissolve it, so that the eggplant is well coated. Set aside to cool.

To form the dumplings, roll the dough into a thick log, then cut into 6 equal pieces. On a lightly dusted board, roll out a piece of dough to roughly 12 cm (5 in) diameter. Don't use too much flour or it will be difficult to close your dumpling. Use your fingers to pinch the edges a little so they are slightly thinner than the rest of the dough.

Place a tablespoon of filling in the middle of the dough and fold the edges over every 2 cm (¾ in) or so to meet in the middle. Flip the dumpling over and, on the floured board, shape the dumpling by flattening it a little. Make sure the folds have closed and leave on the board, fold-side-down, while you make the rest.

Heat a frying pan with a tight-fitting lid over medium heat. Pour in some vegetable oil to coat the bottom of the pan and add the dumplings. Fry for about 2 minutes on each side until golden brown. Add about 60 ml (¼ cup) water and place the lid on immediately. The water should simmer rapidly and create steam that finishes the cooking. Cook for 6–7 minutes until the water has completely evaporated. Remove the lid, flip the dumplings over and crisp them up by cooking for another minute on either side in the dry pan. Serve immediately.

Cooked oyaki keep well for a couple of days in an airtight container in the fridge and can be reheated on a dry (or lightly oiled) pan over medium heat.

Continued ›

ほうとう鍋

HOTO NOODLE SOUP

HOTOUNABE

This noodle hotpot is like a giant hearty miso soup, but filled with a variety of winter vegetables, such as kabocha pumpkin, daikon and napa cabbage, and, most importantly, comfortingly thick hoto noodles that are cooked directly in the pot.

These flat, thick, chewy noodles hail from Yamanashi prefecture, famous for its multiple beautiful views of Mount Fuji. Wheat was introduced to this prefecture when there were food shortages and farmers grew it wherever rice could not be grown. Since poor wheat farming communities (ironically) had little precious flour, this soup contains a lot more vegetables and tofu than noodles, but still manages to be incredibly filling.

Although similar to udon noodles, hoto noodles are unique in that they are wider and flatter. They can be difficult to find outside the region, but are easy to make at home, and if you don't feel like making them, simply use udon noodles. What makes this dish different to other Japanese noodle soups is that the hoto noodles are cooked directly in the pot – this adds starch to the soup, which is already quite thick from the pumpkin. It's a wonderfully hearty meal to warm you up inside and out on a cold day.

SERVES 4

200 g (1⅔ cups) plain (all-purpose) flour
100 ml (3½ fl oz) water
2 litres (8 cups) kombu dashi (page 108)
1 tablespoon sake
1 tablespoon mirin
250 g (9 oz) kabocha pumpkin, diced
⅓ carrot, sliced
5 cm (2 in) piece of daikon, sliced
1 spring onion (scallion), finely sliced
2 tablespoons miso
60 g (2 oz) shimeji mushrooms
4 fresh shiitake mushrooms
100 g (3½ oz) napa cabbage
80 g (2¾ oz) aburaage (fried tofu)

To make the noodles, put the flour and water in a large bowl. Stir together into a shaggy dough, then knead on a clean, dry surface for 10–15 minutes. This takes elbow grease, but you don't have to move fast; just keep kneading until it's very smooth and soft. Cover with a damp tea towel or place in an airtight container and leave to rest for at least 30 minutes.

Roll out the dough into a 2 mm (⅛ in) thick rectangle on a lightly dusted surface, ideally wood. (If it is retracting as you roll, the dough might need another 10 minutes to rest.)

Lightly dust the dough rectangle with flour, then roll it or fold it over itself, dusting with flour between folds. With a large sharp knife, cut it into 1 cm (½ in) thick slices, then unroll carefully and dust the freshly cut noodles in flour.

Put the kombu dashi in a large pot with the sake and mirin. Add the pumpkin, carrot, daikon and white part of the spring onion (save the green part to garnish). Simmer over medium heat for about 10 minutes until the pumpkin begins to soften. In the meantime, put the miso in a small bowl and dilute with some of the soup stock.

Add the rest of the vegetables to the soup pot along with the tofu and noodles and cook for 7–8 minutes (taste a noodle to check: it should no longer taste like raw flour, but still have a good chew). Remove from the heat and stir in the miso. Serve immediately, scattered with the green spring onion.

野菜カレーうどん

VEGETABLE UDON CURRY

YASAI KARE UDON

As in many Japanese families, we had curry regularly growing up. It was the standard Japanese curry made of potatoes, onion, carrot and pork, usually thickened with S&B Golden Curry blocks. It made a weekly appearance in our house and now I regularly make Japanese curry for my own family, too. However, my kids are a little fussy. One likes it with tonkatsu on top and the other doesn't want any meat at all. I began making a curry with no meat in it, but more vegetables, so I only had to make one version. (And whoever wants to add tonkatsu can do so!)

Since making Tuscany my home, it has been arguably harder to get curry blocks. Not impossible, but difficult enough that I realised it was easier to reach for a jar of curry powder and make the curry from scratch. I haven't used a curry block since. If you've got curry blocks, go ahead and use them, but now I use Japanese S&B curry powder, which is very mild and fragrant. You could also use garam masala, or combine the two. The beauty of homemade curry is you can put whatever you like in it, and I can guarantee you that every household in Japan makes their own version. A splash of soy sauce and a bit of miso is what gives a boost of umami to this one.

Udon curry is a great dish to make if you have (as I often do) impatient people who cannot wait the extra 20 minutes or so it takes to make rice (if you have fresh or frozen noodles, this is even faster). You could also serve this with rice, but use half the quantity of dashi – it's just slightly soupier for the noodles.

If you don't have a Japanese grater for ginger (oroshigane), use a microplane.

SERVES 4

2 tablespoons butter
4 cm (1½ in) knob of fresh ginger, finely grated
1 onion, sliced
½ eggplant (aubergine), diced
pinch of salt
1 carrot, peeled and chopped into chunky slices
200 g (7 oz) potato, peeled and chopped
1 tablespoon Japanese curry powder
2 teaspoons garam masala
2 tablespoons mirin (or sake)
1 litre (4 cups) dashi (pages 108–9)
1 tablespoon soy sauce
½ green bell pepper (capsicum), thinly sliced
2 teaspoons potato starch (or cornstarch)
2 tablespoons miso
4 servings udon noodles

Melt the butter in a heavy-based saucepan or donabe over medium heat and stir in the ginger, onion, eggplant and salt.

Stir to coat everything in the buttery ginger for about 2 minutes, being careful the onion doesn't burn, then add the carrot and potato. Tip in the curry powder and garam masala and stir to coat the vegetables.

Pour in the mirin – followed quickly by the dashi. Bring to a simmer and let the vegetables cook for about 10 minutes or until tender. Add the capsicum and cook for a couple of minutes.

Meanwhile, make a slurry by mixing the potato starch with a splash of water until dissolved. Stir into the curry, along with the miso, and let it bubble and thicken for a minute.

Cook the udon noodles following the packet instructions (fresh, dry or frozen). Drain and rinse under cold water to give them a bit of spring.

Distribute the noodles into bowls and pour the vegetable curry over them.

秋茄子は嫁に食わすな

Don't let your daughter-in-law eat your autumn eggplants

This Japanese proverb is so old that no one remembers its exact meaning anymore, but there are two main interpretations. One is that the end-of-season autumn eggplants (aubergines) are so delicious that your ungrateful daughter-in-law doesn't deserve to eat them – the mother-in-law had better keep them for herself!

It is traditional for the daughter-in-law to move in with her husband's family, so this is a bit of a joke that plays on the stereotypical conflict between a new bride and her mother-in-law.

The other interpretation is a reference to the ancient knowledge that eggplants have properties that help reduce your body temperature, which would not be good for a young woman (especially one who could potentially be pregnant) in the cooler autumn days. In this case, the advice to not let your daughter-in-law eat your eggplants is directed at a concerned and thoughtful grandmother-to-be.

Either way, the thing that I love about this phrase is that it passes on knowledge of seasonal foods; in this case, akinasu, autumn eggplant, which is at its peak during the period known as *zansho*, 残暑 ('lingering heat') or autumn equinox. This moment arrives as one of the 72 microseasons in Japan's calendar – four seasons are just not enough to describe everything that is happening in nature so the calendar is, instead, divided into 72 ko or microseasons, a new season every five days.

The concept was borrowed from the Chinese, but, as they did not always describe the Japanese climate, the calendar was rewritten in 1685 by the court astronomer, Shibukawa Shunkai, who gave them poetic names that sound like lines from a haiku.

Zansho arrives during the season called 天地始粛 *Tenchi hajimete samushi* or 'Heat starts to die down' and it corresponds to the official start of autumn at the end of August and beginning of September.

Perhaps this is the real reason for the phrase: to help us remember that the best moment for eggplants is at the start of autumn.

We see similar knowledge of autumn food in Basho's (1644–1694) most important collection of poetry, *Oku no Hosomichi* (*Narrow Road to the Deep North*), where you will again see the reference to *Zansho*.

Zansho shibashi tegoto ni ryore uri nasubi. 'Heat persists awhile; cook melons, eggplants, each to his liking.' ●

麻婆茄子

MAPO EGGPLANT

MABO NASU

Mabo nasu may sound like a familiar Chinese recipe – you might know mapo tofu, a hearty stewed Chinese tofu and pork dish that is much loved in Japan, too. In this version, eggplant takes the place of tofu and does a similar job of soaking up the delicious sauce. This is a very quick meal to make, so if you're serving with other dishes (steamed rice is a must), make sure they're all ready when you start cooking.

Other than bowls of warm rice as a foil to the rich sauce, I'd also serve this with pickles and simple steamed vegetables for a really satisfying meal. For a vegetarian version, just leave out the ground pork. If you happen to have leftovers, they make a very good filling for dumplings (page 76).

SERVES 4

1 large eggplant (aubergine)
vegetable oil, for frying
2 teaspoons potato starch (or cornstarch)
250 ml (1 cup) water or dashi (for an extra boost of flavour)
2 garlic cloves, grated
3 cm (1 in) knob of ginger, grated
150 g (5½ oz) minced (ground) pork (or chicken)
2 tablespoons sake
2 tablespoons mirin
2 tablespoons soy sauce
1 tablespoon miso

Cut the eggplant into thick slices and then into 4–5 cm (2 in) long pieces (think fat chips). Heat about 3 cm (1 in) vegetable oil in a pan and fry the eggplant for 6–7 minutes until golden brown and a fork slips in easily. You may need to cook in batches. Drain the eggplant on paper towel. Pour out the excess oil and wipe out the pan with paper towel.

Mix the potato starch to a slurry with a bit of the water or dashi. Set aside.

Put the pan back over medium heat. Add the garlic, ginger and pork and fry for about 3 minutes, tossing frequently, until the pork is no longer pink and is just cooked.

Return the eggplant to the pan and pour in the sake, mirin and soy sauce, followed by the slurry and the rest of the water or dashi. Stir until combined and bring it back to a simmer – it should very quickly turn into a lovely thick sauce.

Turn off the heat and add the miso, stirring it in well to dissolve it. Serve immediately.

朴葉味噌

MISO & MUSHROOMS ON A MAGNOLIA LEAF

HOBA MISO

This is a quick, tasty dish if you can find dried magnolia leaves. It is a speciality from the mountainous region of Hida Takayama, an ancient castle town in the northern part of Gifu prefecture that spends long winters buried under snow. Over those long winters, when not many fresh vegetables were growing, the people lived off miso and pickles.

This was a simple peasant dish of the somabito (woodsmen), who would take miso with them to grill on the campfire and eat in the forest, gathering the brown magnolia ('hoba') leaves that fall in autumn to use as plates. Maybe some fern shoots or other foraged greens would go in with the miso; perhaps some mushrooms, or shiso.

The leaves are not only practical – in the past they were used to wrap food – but their antibacterial properties also helped prevent the food from spoiling, and they impart a wonderful woody aroma to the food as it cooks.

Ideally, you do need a flame under here – a barbecue, a shichirin (a portable, Japanese charcoal stove), a camping stove, whatever you have available. I have induction at home and that works, too, with the leaf on top of my cast-iron pan. If you can't get magnolia leaves, you can replicate this with aluminium foil (although you won't get the wonderful magnolia fragrance, sadly).

Traditionally, homemade miso was used. I suggest a strongly flavoured miso for this, such as a red or hatcho miso. You can add beef or another meat, to make more of a meal of it. But, being a homely dish from poor origins, this really can be as simple as just miso, spring onions and mushrooms. Don't fret if you don't have fresh ginger or the sake to hand, just leave them out, but maybe add water or dashi to loosen the sauce a bit.

This needs a bowl of steamed rice as a foil to the rich miso and it also pairs very nicely with a glass of sake – indeed, in Hida, it is often served as a snack to unannounced guests, like offering a cup of tea or coffee in other cultures. Add a few side dishes and pickles to cut through the richness and you have a meal.

SERVES 2–4

1 dried magnolia leaf
150 g (5½ oz) mixed fresh mushrooms
3 generous tablespoons miso
1 tablespoon sake
1 teaspoon sugar
½ teaspoon grated ginger
6 spring onions (scallions), finely chopped

Soak the magnolia leaf in water while you prepare. Clean up the mushrooms as needed – trimming any stems (shiitake mushrooms, for example), wiping with damp paper towel, slicing any large mushrooms into smaller pieces.

Combine the miso, sake, sugar and ginger. Spread over the leaf, then sprinkle with spring onions and the mushrooms.

Place directly over a shichirin or barbecue or on a pan over a flame. As the miso begins to bubble, you can move the mushrooms around to cook everything evenly. Serve the mushrooms as they are, straight off the leaf.

さばの味噌煮

MISO MACKEREL

SABA NO MISONI

This dish tastes like home to me. What I love about it, other than the flashes of nostalgia for my grandmother's kitchen, is that it's the kind of dish you can (and should) prepare a batch of and then enjoy over the next several days, warm or cold. It's good the moment you make it, but, if you can be patient, the next day it's even better. As it cools, the mackerel soaks up that delicious miso–ginger sauce. By the time you rewarm it (or enjoy it cold, as I do in the summer), the fish has had even more time to marinate and the flavours have mingled and it is so good you'll be drinking the sauce left over in the bottom of the dish.

Mackerel is the classic fish for this preparation. This oily fish is naturally rich in flavour, stands up well to the sauce and doesn't fall apart during reheating. The strong miso and ginger sauce also helps mask some of the fishy smell it tends to have – mackerel is not for anyone who feels indifferent about fish, that's for sure! If you want to get into loving mackerel – it is a truly fantastic fish: flavourful, sustainable and full of well-documented health benefits – then this is the best way I can think of. My friend Shihoko describes this dish in her blog, *Chopstick Chronicles*, as 'Japanese people's favourite way to eat this fish'.

VARIATIONS: If you really aren't keen on mackerel, this sauce is so good you should still try it – perhaps with another firm, fleshy fish such as cod, kingfish or sardines. For a vegetarian version, use thick slices of fried eggplant (aubergine) or pumpkin, even potato – anything that will do a good job of soaking up these wonderful flavours.

SERVES 4 as a starter

- 2 small mackerels (about 300 g/10½ oz), skin on, but filleted, large bones removed
- 2 heaped tablespoons miso (see note)
- 2 tablespoons sake
- 1 tablespoon mirin
- splash of soy sauce
- 1 tablespoon sugar (I prefer brown sugar)
- thumb-sized piece of ginger, peeled and cut into matchsticks

Cut each mackerel fillet into 3 or 4 pieces. Blanch in boiling water for 1 minute. Drain and pat dry.

Stir together all the other ingredients in a frying pan – this should have a fairly thick consistency but if you need more liquid, add a splash of water.

Warm over low heat to help dissolve the sugar. Add the fish to the pan and make sure it is completely coated with the sauce. Cover with a lid and simmer gently for about 10 minutes.

Cool a little (the longer you can resist the better – it will keep for up to 3 days in the fridge) before serving with fluffy freshly steamed Japanese rice.

Note: I would suggest a more robust flavoured miso such as red miso; I used flavourful mame miso or whole bean miso for this.

ゆべし

YUBESHI

This ancient delicacy comes from Tenryu, deep in the mountains in the southernmost tip of Nagano, where I travelled to learn how to make them from 80-year-old Hama-san. Whole yuzu fruits are emptied out and filled with a sweet, thick miso and walnut filling. Then they're steamed and dried and left to cure for months. It is an ingenious way to preserve abundant yuzu for a long time.

Like many good fermented foods, this is more delicious the longer it ages. It is usually served with green tea, but, because of its complex savoury flavours, this is something you could have with sake or even a glass of whisky. It would be delicious with a soft goat's cheese and is also sometimes sliced and served in clear soup.

There is an Edo period cookbook, *Ryori Monogatari* (*The Tale of Food*), written in 1643, that describes how to prepare yubeshi, but the recipe is possibly even older. It was, they say, a popular portable food of the samurai, who took these miso-stuffed yuzu with them onto the battlefield.

MAKES 10 yubeshi

10 yuzu
50 g (1¾ oz) walnut halves
330 g (11½ oz) miso
330 g (11½ oz) raw cane sugar
100 g (⅔ cup) plain (all-purpose) or rice flour
1 tablespoon sake
1 tablespoon mirin

Cut a little 'cap' off the top of each yuzu, where the stem is, and set aside for serving. With a spoon, scoop out the juice and flesh of the fruit, keeping the skin perfectly intact. Keep the juice and flesh to make ponzu sauce (page 42).

Finely chop half the walnuts, leaving the rest in larger pieces.

Mix together the miso, sugar, flour, sake, mirin and chopped walnut. Spoon into the hollow yuzu until half full. Push in two or three larger pieces of walnut, then keep filling to three-quarters full (see photo top left). Smooth the tops and put the yuzu caps back on.

Place a cloth in the bottom of a steaming basket. Place the yubeshi on the cloth and steam over gentle heat, covered, for 2 hours, checking the water regularly. You should see that the filling is exploding out of the top and the yuzu skins have slumped and become elastic. Carefully (they are hot: cool them a bit first or use gloves or a tea towel), remove the yuzu and, with a spoon or a thin bamboo spatula, push the filling back into the yuzu or remove any that doesn't fit (see photo top right).

The idea is to reshape them perfectly to the round shape of the original fruit, with a slightly raised top, cap and all. Place them back in the steamer and cook for another hour. If you have particularly large yuzu, it could take longer.

Remove from the steamer, cool and keep in a well-ventilated cool place (this is traditionally done during the yuzu season, which is winter) for 2–3 months, until dark, fragrant and very solid.

At first you need to massage them once a week, removing excess moisture and helping the fruit take on the perfect shape. As they dry and become firmer, once every two weeks is fine. Once they are very firm, they are ready to eat and will keep in an airtight container in the fridge to slow down aging for up to 2 years.

Serve in very thin slices with a lovely green tea such as sencha.

ゆべし：伝統食文化の継承

Yubeshi: Passing on the traditions of an ancient slow food

To learn about yubeshi, I visit Nakai Samurai, one of the scattered villages of Tenryu, a community of 1000 people living throughout the forest, deep in the mountains in the southernmost tip of Nagano, on the border of Aichi and Shizuoka prefectures.

Yubeshi preparation is protected and is passed on through a small number of hands here; it is mainly still made by families in their homes. An association was founded in the 1970s to keep the yubeshi tradition alive in this place that was under threat of being forgotten. It has worked.

We follow the road that snakes alongside the Tenryu river, squeezed in between steep mountainsides until we reach the 'secret tea fields' and then we drive sharply, impossibly, up to the tallest tea field, to the highest house, that backs onto monkey-filled forests (90 per cent of Tenryu is forest) and looks high over the river, nearly 400 metres below. There is Hama-san, the 80-something-year-old tea producer, waiting for us with lunch ready on the table and a big smile. With her are two passionate young women, Yuka Naito and Habana Murasawa, who are helping this quiet tea-picking forest village and its elders to retrain and pass on their traditions.

It is early winter, yuzu season – they are everywhere and so is their perfume. The house is surrounded by yuzu trees, some so tall that even the monkeys can't get to the fruit at the top. We set to work, scooping out the juicy fruit, leaving only the peel, whole except for the little 'cap' we cut off to get the fruit out. The empty yuzu are filled with a thick paste made of miso, honey (or sugar), flour (it can be barley flour, regular wheat flour or even rice flour, which gives it a more mochi-like texture), sake, mirin and chunks of walnuts, which grow around here.

Once filled, the yuzu are to be steamed for a couple of hours, so we go for a walk among the steep, sunny tea fields while we wait. When the yuzu have finished steaming, they are left to cure for months, until they turn deep dark brown and the yuzu and miso essentially become one – a salty-sweet-citrusy cake. Luckily, Hama-san had some from last season that we cut into thin slices and enjoyed with freshly brewed tea leaves.

In the spirit of mottainai, don't throw away anything from a yuzu! You can use the whole fruit. It's rich in vitamins and minerals, in particular vitamin C, which is also excellent for your skin. Yuzu is often added to a bath – taking yuzu baths (yuzuyu, 柚子湯) is an ancient tradition and especially practised on the day of the winter solstice.

Yuka also gave us a recipe for an all-natural facial toner: just steep the seeds in sake or shochu for a couple of days – the seeds turn the liquid thick and viscous, like a gel. Use this as a toner to keep your skin soft and glowing. ●

味噌と胡桃のクッキー

WALNUT MISO COOKIES

KURUMIMISO KUKKI

The first time I had miso and walnut together, I thought, I'd like to taste a sweet version of this. I couldn't get the idea of cookies out of my head – soft, chewy, nutty, not-too-sweet cookies to go with a cup of tea or warm amazake (page 162). And I found them. These are simply moreish cookies.

I basically took my children's favourite chocolate chip cookie recipe and added ground walnuts and miso in place of chocolate. After years of perfecting my household's much-requested soft, chewy cookie, I found the key is to use soft, or even melted, butter and brown sugar.

I use white miso for this, which is less salty. If you're using brown miso, add about half the quantity to start with – you can always taste when you've creamed it with the butter and sugar. (In fact, this is the point when I always taste and think, surely this brown sugar-miso-butter would be delicious on other things too … like toast?)

MAKES 16 cookies

110 g (1 cup) walnut halves
50 g (1¾ oz) white sugar
50 g (1¾ oz) brown sugar
100 g (3½ oz) unsalted butter
1 tablespoon white miso
1 egg
120 g (about 1 cup) plain (all-purpose) flour
1 teaspoon baking powder

Pick out 4 walnut halves and split each one into quarters, so you have one bit for each cookie. Blitz the rest in a food processor or chop finely. Set aside.

Cream together the sugars, butter and miso with beaters. If you're using brown miso, taste to check if you need more.

Add the egg and beat in well. Add the walnuts and beat until combined. Swap to a soft spatula and fold in the flour and baking powder. When well combined, flatten to a disc and place in the freezer for about 10 minutes – this makes the dough firmer and easier to roll into balls.

Preheat the oven to 180°C (350°F) and line a baking tray with baking paper.

Use a tablespoon to scoop walnut-sized (keeping to the theme!) balls of dough. Roll in your hands until smooth and place on the baking tray, leaving about 6 cm (2 in) between them. Push a piece of walnut into the centre of each cookie, flattening them a little.

Bake for 8–10 minutes until golden but still a little soft to the touch (they harden as they cool). Cool completely on a wire rack. (But do steal one: these are wonderful warm!)

Store in an airtight container at room temperature for up to a week (unless they are eaten first).

海藻
SEAWEED

海藻

SEAWEED

'And with the ebbing of the tide, They go cutting jewelled seaweed; From the age of gods An awesome, Jewelled mountain isle.'

KANAMURA, LORD KASA, 726

Seaweed has been an important food in Japan since ancient times – evidence of seaweed collected from prehistoric sites tells us it was a staple long ago. Propagating it for consumption was first recorded in the 11th century, when seaweed was transplanted from Kozushima to the Izu peninsula, and nori culture had its beginnings in 1673.

We can see how integrated seaweed was into early Japanese culture by reading medieval poems. The *Manyoshu*, an important anthology of waka poetry from the eighth century, is full of love poems that refer to seaweed, as is *The Tale of Genji* from the 11th century.

'Alas, she is no more,
whose soul was bent to mine
like the bending seaweed.'

– from the *Manyoshu*, eighth century

As marine biologist Felix Bast, author of *Monostroma: The Jeweled Seaweed for Future* says, 'No civilizations exist in which seaweeds are so much integrated into gastronomy, culture and literature as in Japan, either medieval or modern… Seaweed is not just a vegetable for the Japanese; it stood as an imagery and metaphor to express meanings from "love" to "compassion", "truth" and "sensuality".'

'The world of fisher folk:
Might I hear it from afar?
On the beach at Suma,
Seaweed-salt droplets fell,
For who, if not you…'

– from *The Tale of Genji* by Murasaki Shikibu, early 11th century

Today, it is hard to imagine a Japanese meal without the presence of seaweed – and I don't just mean in sushi rolls. You find it in the everyday foods of Japanese homes, from miso soup, noodles and onigiri, to popular snacks such as senbei (rice crackers). But, most of all, seaweed – kombu, to be specific – is the principal ingredient in dashi stock, the backbone of the entire cuisine.

Seaweed can be dried for easy preservation and transportation; it lasts indefinitely, it's incredibly nutritious and is an environmentally friendly food (including seaweed farms, which are carbon sinks). It's the definition of tasty (read more about how the word umami was coined, page 122) and is incredibly versatile in the kitchen.

I have always wondered why more people aren't eating this superfood outside East Asia. It seems seaweed was once also important in ancient Europe; but, somehow, over thousands of years, many western cultures have forgotten how to eat it, aside from small pockets in places such as Ireland, Scotland and Scandinavia.

When you consider that Japan has one of the world's longest coastlines (30,000 kilometres, nearly 19,000 miles, of it) and reflect on the connection between Japanese culture and the sea, it should come as no surprise that at some point people began eating this abundant sea vegetable.

Perhaps seaweed became so important because of Japan's relatively small amount of arable land. The country is three-quarters mountains – this leaves a very small amount of space for growing crops, most of it designated for rice cultivation.

Or perhaps it was because, for 12 centuries, under the rule of generations of Buddhist emperors, the consumption of red meat was forbidden and the nation's diet consisted of mainly vegetables, rice, soybeans and fish. Consuming dairy, too, was unthinkable until recent times – drinking milk would have been like drinking blood (in fact, many Japanese are lactose intolerant, even today). Perhaps it was a dietary deficiency that prompted the ancient Japanese to begin searching the sea for produce and incorporating seaweed into their meals.

Seaweed is extremely rich in fibre, protein, essential vitamins and minerals, far outdoing land vegetables, grains, meat and fish in nutritional content. It has often been considered a medicinal food: it has been seen to help reduce cholesterol, balance blood sugar, aid intestinal function and boost metabolism and the famed longevity of Japan's elderly population is often attributed to the regular consumption of seaweed.

So, if you are curious about incorporating some seaweed into your everyday meals, I hope you will find inspiration in these pages, from dashi stock to onigiri to salads and even dessert. There are over 100 types of edible seaweed found in Japan, although some estimate that number to be closer to 1500. Outside Japan, however, only a handful of seaweed varieties seem to be available – mainly nori, kombu, wakame, kanten and hijiki – so the recipes here will concentrate on those.

TYPES OF SEAWEED

Kombu

Kombu (*Laminaria japonica*) is the most important of the seaweeds and possibly one of the most ancient of Japanese ingredients. A very large, long, leaf-like kelp, it is sold dried and often ready-cut into squares that conveniently fit in a pot. There about 18 varieties of edible kombu and it is the essential ingredient in dashi stock. We also have kombu to thank for helping us discover the power of umami in 1907 (page 122).

Kombu, which doesn't like warm water, thrives in the cold waters of Hokkaido. Richard Hosking describes the way it is harvested in his *Dictionary of Japanese Food*: 'New growth is not from the stem, but from the tip of the leaf, and it is the second- or third-year growths that are harvested, since they are the best for food.' He also points out that only live kombu is harvested (dead kombu washed up on the shore is no good for eating). This is done in late summer and early autumn from specially made boats. The kombu is then dried on land – it was once sun-dried; today it is finished in air-drying chambers.

Nori

Probably the best known of the seaweeds outside Japan, thanks to sushi, nori (*Porphyra tenera*) hardly needs an introduction. It is used for rolling sushi and onigiri to conveniently allow for the easy eating of Japanese rice, which is rather sticky. It is cut into thin, black strips to top soba noodles, or added in squares to ramen bowls.

To make sheets of nori ready to use in the kitchen, this variety of red algae is turned into a pulp, then spread out and dried on racks, then toasted. Although nori culture had its beginnings in the 1670s, the drying technique was developed in Tokyo during the Edo period, around 1750, inspired by washi paper making. The sheets are made to a standard size of 21 x 19 centimetres (8 x 7½ inches).

While there is a wild nori, **iwanori**, which has a rougher texture, almost all nori today is made from farmed seaweed, an industry made possible by a British scientist, Kathleen Mary Drew-Baker (the 'mother of the sea' to the Japanese). Her seaweed studies in Wales helped rescue the decline in nori after the Second World War.

Nori is called the 'vegetable of the sea' because it is so rich in vitamins, protein and fibre – just one sheet of nori contains the same amount of vitamin C as an egg.

You can also find seasoned nori (**yaki nori** or **ajitsuke nori**), which is salty, slightly spiced and cut into convenient small strips for wrapping around rice or snacking on. There is also a type of nori called **aonori** that is green and dried in sprinkles for topping dishes such as okonomiyaki and noodles, or used as an ingredient in shichimi togarashi spice mix.

What to look for: Good nori should be jet black and shiny, without a purple, or any other, colour tint – these indicate a lesser quality. It should be smooth and have a wonderful, clean aroma. When you taste it, it should be crisp and crunchy, yet dissolve in the mouth.

Keep an eye out for **hatsutsumi nori**, which is from the first harvest, a season that, in the Seto Inland Sea, runs from December to March. This first harvest produces the most prized, tender seaweed that melts on your tongue (unlike kombu, which is best from the second or third harvest).

I visited the Hamada family, well-established nori farmers on Shodo Island, as they were getting ready to collect the first harvest of the season. They collect the newest sprigs of the plant and leave the rest to keep growing. Within about ten days, a second harvest happens, then a third. They can get six to eight harvests from the same plant. When I ask the farmers which they eat, their reply is immediate – *only hatsutsumi!* In their eyes, the later harvests are only suitable to feed to their dogs.

Kanten & Agar

Seaweed can be used even for making sweets and, in particular, it makes a hard-set jelly called kanten. Tengusa (*Gelidiaceae*) is a red algae that is washed, soaked and sun-dried until it loses its colour. It is then simmered and strained and the resulting jelly is called kanten. The story goes that this plant-based gelatin was discovered by accident in the mid-1600s, when an innkeeper found that a pot of the previous night's soup had set.

Kanten is a main ingredient in Japanese confectionery (such as my favourite Japanese treat, yokan, red bean jelly, which requires

THREAD KANTEN
WAKAME
NORI
AONORI
HIJIKI
KOMBU

the best grade). It is full of fibre, virtually free of calories and has long been known as an important health food – the locals' longevity is often attributed to their consumption of kanten. Numerous studies have shown its effectiveness in balancing blood sugar and lowering cholesterol and the risk of diabetes, tumours and cancer. It is also an excellent antioxidant and important for intestine health.

Kanten sets at room temperature rather than fridge temperature, so it's a good jelly to use in hot weather. It's also known as agar agar (although the Japanese do distinguish agar agar and kanten as two different seaweed varieties). See page 104 to learn more about how kanten is produced in the mountains of Nagano.

Hijiki

This dark brown twiggy seaweed grows on rocky coastlines in southern Japan. It has an earthier taste than the other seaweeds mentioned here, almost like a mushroom, and a texture that is similar to cooked grains. It is decidedly un-seaweedy. Unlike the other seaweeds, hijiki (*Hizikia fusiformis*) really suits a rich, flavourful sauce.

Hijiki grows in abundance in the Seto Inland Sea and there is a unique harvest for this seaweed, which is often wild foraged by fishermen as an extra source of income. Here is how it is described in the *Setouchi Cookbook*, a collection of recipes from the Seto Inland Sea collected by producers of the area: 'It's a spring vegetable, which is typically foraged for a few brief days in April by local fishermen, as a fisherman's license is required to harvest it in the Setouchi [Seto Inland Sea]. The conditions can be challenging. The fishermen often have to enter the cold water in the middle of the night if that is when the tide is at its lowest. They then cut the hijiki with small sickles, leaving several inches at the base so that the plant can produce a new crop the following year.' Once harvested, it is washed and dried in the sun, then brought inside to be steamed, then fully dried again for packaging.

You can find fresh or dried hijiki, but the most common is dried. As it is already cooked, you simply need to soak it to rehydrate before adding it to dishes. I love it as a side dish, in a salad (page 126) or even mixed through rice for a speckled onigiri (page 121). There are two parts to this sea plant: nagahijiki, the stem, which looks like long, black, tangled threads; and mehijiki, little pieces of leaf or sprout. The former is crisp and firm; the latter, more tender and mild.

Hijiki is a particularly nutritious seaweed, incredibly rich in iron, magnesium, potassium and calcium – 27 times more iron than spinach and 12 times more calcium than milk. In fact, there is a saying in Japan: 'Those who eat hijiki live longer.'

There might be concerns about the fact that some western countries have prohibited the sale of hijiki over the presence of inorganic arsenic, which is absorbed through heavy metals in seawater and can be toxic in very large quantities. But, don't panic! The amount of hijiki anyone would eat is nowhere near enough to have a toxic effect; in fact, the Japanese Bureau of Public Health has never had a single report of arsenic poisoning due to eating hijiki – and this in a seaweed-loving country where hijiki is eaten every day by millions of Japanese. In addition, a 2018 study by Korean scientists showed that cooking hijiki for even 5 minutes removes up to 80 per cent of any arsenic content. The Japanese Bureau of Public Health recommends eating no more than 5 g (¼ oz) of hijiki per day to safely consume this delicious seaweed regularly.

Where to be extremely cautious, on the other hand, is with seaweed supplements. These pills contain extremely concentrated doses that equate to an amount of fresh seaweed that wouldn't be natural to eat.

Wakame

Wakame (*Undaria pinnatifida*) is one of the better known seaweeds outside Japan. This lovely, deep jade-hued seaweed has been eaten by the Japanese since at least the Nara period – it is even mentioned in the *Manyoshu*, an eighth century anthology of Japanese poetry – although it is mostly all farmed now in Japan.

Mild and sweet, faintly reminiscent of the sea, you'll find wakame in miso soup, noodles, tempura and salads. This is another good one for hot summer days – silky and slippery and easy to eat – and is especially refreshing in one of my favourite salads with cucumber and ginger (page 118).

Making kanten in the mountains of Nagano

Kanten is a freeze-dried vegetable gelatin made from tengusa seaweed (*Gelidiaceae*). It was curious to me that I had to travel to Nagano, a landlocked region known for its mountainous terrain and harsh winters, to understand more about how it is made. But I discovered that it is because of this area's natural resources that kanten production was introduced to Nagano around 200 years ago.

The Irisen Kanten farm in Chino, Nagano, sits at about 1000 metres (3300 feet) above sea level in the foothills of the volcanic Yatsugatake mountain range. Winters here are cold and dry, but also sunny, and, thanks to the altitude, there is a big difference between day and night temperatures, which is vital for the dehydration of the kanten. The area is blessed with an abundance of mountain spring water from nearby Mount Tateshina, which is vital for washing and boiling the seaweed.

During the long winters, farmers found it difficult to make an income, so they developed this freeze-drying method for preserving tofu and daikon, which grows in abundance in the cold, frosty winters here. They realised it would also work well for kanten, which was being produced in a similar way in Kyoto.

Kanten is said to be the first food that was made in Japan – many of Japan's most important traditional foods were brought from China or Korea. To understand kanten's invention, however, you need to first know about tokoroten, a favourite snack of cold jelly noodles that was the epitome of fancy dining during the Edo period. Tengusa seaweed was boiled and the liquid then strained into trays; the liquid set and the resulting jelly was pushed through a wooden contraption called a tensuki that cut it into long square-cut noodles. These were then dressed in sauces – sweet or savoury, according to regional tastes.

Tokoroten noodles were made for the nobility, often as a gift for the Shogun. Legend has it that in the mid-1600s Lord Shimazu of the Satsuma clan was travelling from Edo and stayed at an inn called Minoya in Fushimi, on the outskirts of Kyoto, where he ate tokoroten. It was winter. The innkeeper, Tarozaemon, threw out the leftovers and they froze overnight. The next day they defrosted and dehydrated, until, after several nights and days of freezing and defrosting, the tokoroten had turned dry and white. Tarozaemon, curious, decided to boil them and noticed that the liquid became a firm, translucent jelly when cool. He called it 'dried tokoroten' and began serving this new food to his customers, who received it enthusiastically.

One day a group of Buddhist monks from Manpuku-ji temple in Kyoto arrived and, after tasting this new dish, they asked what it was called. Since Tarozaemon hadn't yet given it a name, one of the monks suggested kanten, 寒天, which comes from the kanji characters for 'cold or freezing' (*kan*) and 'sky, heavenly or day' (*ten*).

The idea of producing freeze-dried kanten arrived in Nagano in the 1800s, when a farmer from Chino went to Kyoto and learned the art of kanten-making. Realising the climate back in his homeland was not only similar but had the potential to be even better for kanten production, he brought the techniques back with him.

To show off what they could do in Nagano with their colder winters, the new makers chose to make a long, thick bar shape, called bo kanten (stick kanten), rather than the ito kanten (thread kanten) similar to the dried tokoroten noodles. You need -8°C (18°F) to freeze a bar shape, compared to -2°C (28°F) to freeze the thin threads.

Nagano is one of only two places producing naturally made kanten in Japan today. Kanten was also introduced to Gifu prefecture in the Showa era (1926–1989) and is made there essentially just as it was in the 1600s, in the form of freeze-dried ito kanten.

Today, industrially made agar – made with a different type of seaweed (*gracilaria*), conveniently in powder form and, also conveniently, not dependent on the climate or the season – has taken over from naturally made kanten in the country. Only 15 producers remain, according to the Tokyo Foundation: it seems the art of kanten-making might be on the verge of disappearing.

Continued ›

THE ARTISANAL KANTEN PROCESS

In Chino, Nagano, we meet Chino-san (yes, he has the same name as the town he lives in) at his family's farm, Irisen Kanten, where he has taken over his family's 80-year-old kanten-making process. They begin making in late December, as the outdoor temperature needs to be -8°C (18°F) or lower for the jelly to freeze all the way through. During the day, under the winter sun, the bars sit out in the field on bamboo racks. They melt, dehydrating as they freeze again overnight, then melt during the day – always freezing and melting.

'This shape of kanten you can only do in this area,' explains Chino, proudly, showing me a packet of ito kanten (string kanten) made in Gifu. Most Japanese, Chino-san says, are familiar with the powder form but have no idea how kanten is produced. 'Powder is more convenient, sure,' he says, but he continues to make these bars of kanten because there are still 'people who care that they are made naturally, dried in sun, in traditional way'. It is a laborious process (and at the mercy of the changing weather) that comes from the knowledge and old tools of his ancestors and the natural resources around them: the free-flowing, natural spring water coming off Mount Tateshina, the freezing, dry air and the sun.

'You can't make this in a factory: you need the sunlight,' he says, pulling out several pots full of fluffy, dried seaweed of varying colours – red, beige, white, yellow – pigments that fade after washing and drying. Today, these come from Indonesia, Spain, Portugal and Korea, to name a few. But traditionally in Japan, tengusa came from Izu Shimoda and Shizuoka. It was hand-harvested from under rocks by the ama, literally 'women of the sea', divers who collected pearls, shellfish and seaweed. The seaweed was dried on the beach before being brought by horseback over the mountain. Once the railways were built in the Showa period, transport was easier, as was importing seaweed from other places. Today, most of it comes from abroad.

They work on 300 kilograms (660 pounds) of seaweed to make 10,000 sticks each day. They live and work here for the season, which starts in late December (or once the temperatures get low enough) and they finish around 10 February – although it used to be 20 March. Global warming is making it harder to continue making kanten, as the season is getting shorter and shorter.

They spend one entire day just washing the seaweed with fresh mountain water, spinning it through huge metal washers for around ten hours. Before these machine washers were invented, Chino's ancestors washed the seaweed by hand in the freezing rivers. The seaweed then goes into pools to soak for two more days to remove any bitterness.

The next step is boiling the seaweed. Chino-san uses a three-metre (ten-foot) deep cedar wood-lined iron pot. His family has used this same wooden barrel for over 80 years. It takes about nine hours for the water to come to the boil in the enormous pot because it is absolutely freezing in the open-air shed. The seaweed goes in and takes about three hours to boil. Then the fire goes off and the massive amounts of boiled seaweed are strained in giant cloths. All the seaweed extract needs to be squeezed out, so weights of custom-made wood are placed on top, while the liquid is captured in a pool underneath. The jelly is quickly transferred to long shallow trays to set. They have to work fast – kanten begins to set at room temperature, so they don't have long to work in the freezing air. In fact, ideally they want to be doing this during the warmest part of the afternoon, so this gruelling day of boiling seaweed begins at 1am.

The jelly is then cut with a long comb and the resulting long wobbly bars, called namaten, are placed directly out in the sunlit fields, laid in rows on straw mats. Finally the namaten are punctured all over with a nail-studded instrument. These holes help them defrost more evenly and preserve their shape.

Once the kanten is dehydrated and has turned white, it is placed between two beautiful bamboo racks. These are stacked, still outside, to dry completely – a process that takes about two weeks.

The bamboo racks, I discover, are recycled objects from Chino-san's ancestors, who once reared silkworms for raw silk, which was reeled by hand. They used these racks for keeping the cocoons. He inherited 3500 of these trays and uses them now for drying fruit and vegetables as well as the kanten.

In the little farm shop next door I buy some kanten for just 350 yen or 2 euro for a packet of two long, thick bars, to take home with me to Italy. Using 80- to 200-year-old tools, and nothing else but what nature has gifted this area, they are working for hours at a time, every single day, washing, boiling and straining jelly for 'people who care'. Because they can; because it is something that can only be made here, in this exact spot.

'The cold, the spring water, sunny days, the tools … These are the four main reasons this area became known for kanten,' says Chino-san. 'There aren't a lot of places in Japan that have all this.'

昆布だし

KOMBU DASHI

This is not only the easiest recipe in the world, but it is one of the best-kept secret ingredients ever. All you need is a piece of kombu (dried kelp), which keeps very well in the pantry, and cold water. Put the kombu in the water and forget about it until the next day. Your kombu dashi is done.

Of course, if you're like me and you don't always plan ahead, you can also make kombu dashi on the spot in 10 minutes by heating it very gently until it almost boils – the idea is to draw out, as slowly as possible, the flavour of the kombu. (It is still the easiest recipe in the world.) This differs from regular dashi in that it contains no katsuobushi (dried bonito flakes), making it suitable for vegetarians and vegans too.

Kombu usually comes dried in pieces that have been cut to an easy length to fit in a packet. If you don't need much, you can always cut the dry pieces in half with scissors. For this quantity of dashi, you only need a piece about 12 cm (5 in) long. As it rehydrates, it will swell to its full size. If it's summertime, you may want to keep this in the fridge, but in winter you can leave it out.

Interestingly, the type of water you use has an effect on the resulting kombu dashi. If you are in an area of hard water (rich in minerals, such as calcium and magnesium), or are using bottled water, which tends to be hard, this will result in cloudy dashi, because of an interaction with the calcium in the water. This is not a big deal if you are making miso soup or curry, for example, but if you want a very clear soup, that can be a problem. Soft water (such as Tokyo tap water) will not only make the clearest dashi, but also have a stronger umami flavour and less bitterness.

MAKES 500 ml (2 cups) dashi

1 piece of kombu about 12 cm (5 in) long
500 ml (2 cups) cold water

Cold infusion method: Put the kombu in the cold water, cover (use a jar with a lid if putting in the fridge) and leave overnight to infuse. The next morning, remove the kombu and save it for making tsukudani (page 110). The dashi is now ready to use.

Heating method: If you don't have time for the cold infusion, simply place the kombu and water in a saucepan over low heat so it warms up and draws out the flavour as slowly as possible. Just before it starts to boil, remove from the heat and remove the kombu. Your dashi is ready.

一番だし

FIRST-BREWED DASHI

ICHIBAN DASHI

Ichiban dashi is the go-to dashi, the backbone of Japanese home cooking. It is not only indispensable, but it is an ancient preparation, dating to the seventh century. Today, many people choose to use the convenient powder form of dashi, but this is extremely quick to make – no trickier than brewing a cup of tea.

Although kombu dashi (opposite) is the easiest to make, simply adding a handful of katsuobushi flakes to it will have a powerful synergistic effect on your dashi stock – it enhances the umami by an incredible eight times, giving that characteristic flavour of Japanese cooking.

MAKES 500 ml (2 cups) dashi

500 ml (2 cups) kombu dashi (opposite)
10 g (1 cup) katsuobushi flakes

After removing the kombu, put your dashi in a pan and bring to a simmer over medium–high heat. Remove from the heat – you do not want it to boil – then add the katsuobushi. Leave to infuse for 5–10 minutes.

Strain the dashi through a fine-meshed sieve. You can save the kombu and katsuobushi for a second brew, or to make niban dashi (below). These leftovers can be frozen or kept in the fridge for a couple of days at most; they do not keep well for long periods once soaked.

The dashi is now ready to use. It can be stored in the fridge for up to a week, or in the freezer for 3 months.

VARIATIONS OF DASHI

Since there is **ichiban dashi**, there is also **niban dashi** (second brewed dashi), made by simply saving the kombu and katsuobushi from the first brew and brewing for a second time. This is a perfect no-waste preparation: there is no sense in wasting the ingredients of the first brew, which can easily be frozen to use again.

Niban dashi, as you might imagine, is not as powerful as the first brew, but is useful for dishes where you don't need the dashi to be the primary flavour (miso soup, for example). If you would like a little more flavour, you can add extra kombu and katsuobushi to the niban dashi.

Dashi can be made from other things, too. My obaachan would make dashi from **niboshi**, which are tiny dried anchovies or sardines and very typical of where she came from in southern Japan. **Dried shiitake mushrooms** make a wonderful vegetarian or vegan form of dashi, with a very special flavour and aroma.

昆布の佃煮

KOMBU SIMMERED WITH SOY & MIRIN

KOMBU NO TSUKUDANI

Tsukudani is a technique for preserving seaweed, seafood or vegetables by simmering in sweet soy sauce and mirin sauce. It's one of the most beloved Japanese condiments, particularly around Tokyo – in fact, it is named after the place where the technique originated, Tsukuda Island, a small fishing island in Tokyo Bay, with 'ni' meaning simply simmered or boiled. It didn't take long for this to become a speciality and symbol of Edo, old Tokyo.

I love tsukudani made with kombu – it is not only a umami bomb, perfect for adding to plain rice as a condiment, but it is also an excellent way to use up the kombu that's left over from making dashi. I never throw away this kombu; even if I don't have time, there and then, to make tsukudani, I will just freeze it until I can make a batch. If you've used katsuobushi in your dashi, you can also add this to the tsukudani.

You can add other ingredients for flavour or texture too, such as tiny dried fish, finely chopped ginger, walnuts, sesame seeds or chilli flakes, burdock or lotus root, and even other types of seaweed, such as wakame or nori, which will basically turn it into a paste.

There is also an unusual type of tsukudani that came about in rural Japan during times of food shortages and features locust larvae. As you can see, there are really no rules when it comes to this type of preserving – it is about using what you have.

One thing I have noticed when making this at home is that the type and quality of kombu used makes a huge difference to the outcome. The thicker the kombu, the better and more 'juicy' it will be. Very thin or old kombu tends to be tough and will dry out very quickly – if you discover this is happening, add a little more vinegar, which helps soften the kombu. And don't allow all the liquid in the pan to evaporate, as described in the recipe – the kombu will soak this up and be less dry and tough.

This can easily be multiplied – I have given the measurements for a leftover piece of kombu from making dashi. This makes a really small amount but it's enough for several servings to top steamed rice, it's perfect also on ochazuke (page 246).

SERVES 4

1 piece of kombu, soaked
2 teaspoons mirin
2 teaspoons sugar
2 teaspoons soy sauce
1 teaspoon rice vinegar
60 ml (¼ cup) water

Slice the kombu into very thin matchsticks, or chop into tiny squares. Stir in a small saucepan with all the other ingredients and bring to a gentle simmer over low–medium heat. As it's such a small amount, don't walk away from the pan: it can reduce quickly and burn. Also, try not to stir – splashing soy sauce around the side of the pan can lead to burning. Just watch it simmer down until almost no liquid is left. Put in a jar and keep in the fridge. It keeps well for 1–2 weeks.

鰹節

Katsuobushi

Katsuobushi (鰹節) deserves a special section in this book. It's such an important and fascinating ingredient – with a long history and unique flavour and aroma – that I almost gave it its own chapter, along with other dried foods such as shiitake mushrooms and baby anchovies.

Katsuobushi is always in my pantry and goes hand in hand with kombu to make classic ichiban dashi (page 109), but it is also a condiment in its own right – it's a delicious topping for chilled tofu, miso soup, rice and the easiest side dishes, blanched spinach with a splash of soy sauce, for example.

Although it only spends a few minutes in the dashi stock (just like making a cup of tea, you simply infuse katsuobushi in hot water, off the heat), this is enough to release its powerful, yet elegant, flavour.

The method for making katsuobushi dates back four centuries to the Edo period. Fillets of protein-rich bonito (katsuo) or skipjack tuna are dried, smoked and cured until perfectly rock hard, like blocks of wood. The bonito is shaved with a special tool called a kezuriki, which is rather like a mandolin on top of a wooden box with a drawer. The paper-thin slices shaved from the bonito block drop into the drawer underneath.

My mother remembers using this method for katsuobushi when she was a child in the 1960s; now, most people buy convenient packages of shaved katsuobushi and it's mainly chefs who still use the kezuriki.

To make the dried blocks of bonito, the fish is first cleaned, filleted, simmered and then deboned. The next step is to dry it. In some places, such as the southern port town of Makurazaki in Kyushu (one of the most famous areas for katsuobushi), the tuna is dried out in the sun for a few months, even up to a year. In other places, the drying is done by smoking the fillets, or smoke-drying, known as baikan. The smoked fillets, at this point, are known as arabushi and can be found in this form, too, ready for use in dashi. This version is a bit more affordable than the highest grade katsuobushi that has gone through the entire process and is known as honkarebushi.

Honkarebushi undergoes a lengthy process of fermentation (up to four different ferments), alternated with sun-drying, for several months until the hard blocks of premium bonito are ready. The moulds introduced for the ferment can differ, but at one time koji mould was used. This part of the process was only introduced in the 1700s, to make the katsuobushi more transportable and help it last longer – by introducing 'good' mould, the 'bad' mould wouldn't grow.

Bonito blocks look like carved pieces of old wood covered in a fine layer of sawdust. They are available from specialist stores, from honkarebushi producers or online. If you want to try one for freshly shaved katsuobushi, remember you will need the kezuriki (or a mandolin) to shave it. As you might imagine, honkarebushi keep well for a very long time. ●

湯豆腐

SIMMERED TOFU

YUDOFU

Don't be deceived by the simplicity of this recipe – it is so comforting, yet elegant and nourishing and satisfying. I am confident that what you're experiencing when you eat this warm hug of a dish is the chemistry and magic of umami that happens when kombu dashi and silky tofu come together.

I like this with silken tofu, which can be a bit delicate to handle, not to mention tricky to get out of the container unless you know this secret… Take the plastic off the top of the container and flip it upside down onto a plate (or directly into the pot in this case). With sharp scissors, snip a tiny bit off each of the four corners (be sure to find and discard them). You should now be able to lift off the container with ease.

SERVES 2

250 g (9 oz) silken tofu

375 ml (1½ cups) kombu dashi (page 108)

sesame seeds; soy sauce; chopped chives, spring onion (scallion) or garlic chives; grated ginger; ponzu sauce (page 43); katsuobushi, to serve (optional)

Place the silken tofu in a saucepan and cover with the kombu dashi. Bring to a simmer for about 2 minutes until heated through.

Slice into 2 pieces and serve in bowls with the kombu dashi. Serve with any, or none, of the suggested accompaniments.

昆布締め

KOMBU-CURED SASHIMI

KOBUJIME

Sashimi is not only for restaurants; it is often served at home because it is so easy and quick – just slice some fresh fish and put it on the table. However, this one little tweak will make all the difference.

Kobujime is an effortless technique that imparts incredible flavour and texture to sashimi, thanks to the umami power of kombu. Simply sandwich the fresh fish between kombu for 24 hours before serving.

It sounds like something modern, invented by a chef, but kobujime came about during the time of Japan's isolation in the Edo period (1603–1868). Merchant ships known as the kitamae-bune travelled up and down the Sea of Japan, buying and selling goods, back and forth between Osaka and Hokkaido, via the Seto Inland Sea. They transported sake, salt, rice, kombu and silk, among many other things, but they also transported culture along the coastline, sharing folk songs and weaving techniques, for example, and, of course, food.

During the months-long voyages, fish caught in Toyama Bay, in central Japan, would be wrapped in Hokkaido kombu to preserve it. As the fish aged and absorbed the umami, it became richer and more delicious. Hokkaido's kombu is still used all over Japan today.

VARIATIONS: Traditionally, this technique was used for swordfish, but also squid, shellfish and prawns from Toyama (prawn kobujime is a speciality of the prefecture). Today you will find it with any white fish, such as snapper, sea bream and flounder. Vegans, this is a wonderful way to impart flavour to vegetables, too. Try cucumber or lightly blanched or grilled peppers (capsicums), eggplant (aubergine) or okra.

SERVES 2–3

about 6 pieces of kombu
1 whole sea bass (around 800 g/1 lb 12 oz) or 2 fillets (around 500 g/1 lb 2 oz)
soy sauce, radish slices and wasabi, to serve (optional)

Rehydrate the kombu by soaking in water for at least 30 minutes while you prepare the fish.

If you are filleting the fish yourself, first make a diagonal slice to remove the head, following the opening of the gills. From here, cut the first fillet by locating the backbone and, using the spine as a guide, cut all the way along the fish to the tail and pull out the first fillet. Flip the fish over and repeat. You can use the off-cuts to make a fish stock. Gently run the fillets under cold water and pat dry.

Drain and pat dry the kombu. Place half the kombu on a tray, cover with a layer of sea bass fillets and then cover with the second layer of kombu. Wrap in plastic or in a resealable bag, pushing out the air. Put a weight on top, such as a board and some jars or tins, and leave to cure for 24 hours.

Unwrap, remove the kombu (use it for tsukudani, page 110) and cut the fish into thick slices, slightly on the diagonal. Serve with soy sauce, radish and wasabi, if you like; however, I recommend tasting it first, just as it is, to enjoy the full flavour of the kombu-infused sashimi.

茶わん蒸し

TEACUP STEAMED CUSTARDS

CHAWANMUSHI

Silky, savoury chawanmushi is a very special dish, usually eaten as part of a larger kaiseki (traditional, multi-course) meal. This is something I only ate in restaurants or ryokan while I was growing up, but it is not difficult to make at home. Cooked in little teacups with a lid, it is very gently steamed for the perfect quiver and melt-in-the-mouth texture.

This is a great example of the omnipresence of seaweed in important Japanese dishes. The kombu dashi here – which needs to be perfectly in proportion to the eggs in a one to three ratio – is one of the most important parts of the recipe. Even though you cannot see it, it is what gives this extremely delicate dish its umami.

There are a variety of ingredients inside the custard that you discover, like buried treasure, once you begin eating. Pieces of chicken thigh, prawn, decorative carrot slices, shiitake mushrooms (try shimeji or another kind), ginkgo nuts (my favourite), kamaboko (fish cakes) and mitsuba (Japanese parsley) are all very traditional – add any you like. As I love the custard more than anything else, I try not to overcrowd it too much.

If you are using dried rather than fresh shiitake mushrooms, soak them in hot water for an hour before beginning (strain the liquid and use it to make up your kombu dashi).

SERVES 4

2 large eggs (55 g/2 oz each), at room temperature
300 ml (10 fl oz) kombu dashi (page 108)
1 teaspoon usukuchi soy sauce (or regular soy sauce)
1 teaspoon mirin
2 shiitake mushrooms, finely sliced
2 large fresh prawns, peeled and chopped into 2–3 cm/1 in pieces
4 mitsuba sprigs or finely chopped chives

It helps to bring everything to room temperature before you begin, in particular the eggs and dashi.

Beat the eggs in a bowl and pass through a strainer into a large jug. Add the kombu dashi, soy sauce and mirin.

If you don't have chawanmushi cups with lids, use ramekins or teacups. Place a few mushroom slices and pieces of prawn in each cup. Pour in the egg mixture and top with mitsuba (if you're using chives, add once it is cooked). Put the lids on or cover with foil.

Prepare a steamer with a lid. Place the cups carefully inside and steam on the lowest heat, covered, for 15–20 minutes. They should be very wobbly on top, but, if you poke them, you should see the liquid is clear.

Carefully remove the cups (they will be very hot!), keeping the lids on so they keep warm. Serve with spoons.

SOME TIPS ON STEAMING CHAWANMUSHI

The excellent blog *Just One Cookbook* by Nami Chen has some good tips. She cooks hers in a large casserole dish using the bain marie method: she puts the custards with their lids inside the dish, half-fills the dish with water and puts the lid on.

If you are using a bamboo steamer, it might not be quite tall enough. If you find your cups don't fit in the steamer with the lids on, cover them with tin foil instead. You can also wrap the steamer lid with a tea towel to stop any condensation dripping into the custards; this is a tip from another favourite Japanese food blog of mine, *RecipeTin Japan* by Yumiko Maehashi.

海藻サラダ

SEAWEED SALAD

KAISOU SALADA

This simple side dish belongs in a category called 'sunomono', which describes vegetable dishes dressed with vinegar, a popular preparation in Japanese home cooking. It's a gentle, easy-to-make salad. If you can only find wakame, just use wakame, but if you can find a variety of different dried seaweeds they will add to the texture, colour and flavour of this dish. Try arame, thread agar, dulse, hijiki, gagome or green kelp, for example.

This is particularly refreshing in the summer months and is also delicious as a topping for cold soba noodles or chilled tofu. If you want to build on this salad, you could add shredded poached crab or chicken, prawns or even shirasu, tiny dried anchovies (my obaachan's favourite).

SERVES 2–3

10 g (¼ oz) mixed dried seaweeds, such as arame, wakame and hijiki
½ long cucumber
1 teaspoon salt
3–4 radishes, thinly sliced
2 cm (¾ in) piece of ginger, grated
1 tablespoon rice vinegar
½ tablespoon raw (demerara) sugar
1 teaspoon soy sauce
½ teaspoon toasted sesame seeds

Soak the seaweed in water for 10 minutes to rehydrate it. Check the packet directions for rehydrating wakame: it usually only needs to soak but some brands might ask you to blanch it too.

Meanwhile, partially peel the cucumber in long strips, then thinly slice. Place in a bowl with the salt, toss to combine and then leave for about 5 minutes – the excess liquid should collect at the bottom of the bowl. Drain and rinse the cucumber and pat dry with paper towel.

Drain the seaweed, squeezing out any excess water, and arrange on a plate with the cucumber and radish.

Stir together the ginger, vinegar, sugar and soy sauce. Give it a taste: it shouldn't taste too acidic (if so, add a little more sugar) or too sweet (add a touch more vinegar). Once the sugar has dissolved, drizzle it over the seaweed and sprinkle with sesame seeds. Serve at once, or chill and serve within a day.

ひじきおにぎり

HIJIKI ONIGIRI

The shape of this onigiri is called tawara gata (俵型), referencing a bale of rice – the rice was formed into cylindrical bales that were easy for farmers to carry on their shoulders from the rice fields. My grandmother used to make this, instead of the better known triangle onigiri – it's very quick and easy to shape, and fits perfectly into bento boxes.

Hijiki is a popular filling for onigiri and, although I love the simplicity of this speckled look, you could add one or two other ingredients here for some colour, such as blanched and podded edamame, or julienned carrots (which you can simmer together in the sauce).

It can be difficult to measure hijiki because it's a dried tangle and doesn't fit into spoons or cups – it's also too light for weighing accurately; to give you an idea, 10 grams (¼ oz) of dried hijiki will grow to about a cup of rehydrated hijiki. That is double what you need for this recipe, so, with any left over, try making the dressing on page 126.

MAKES 6

2 cups (about 400 g) freshly cooked rice (page 36)
pinch of salt
1 nori sheet

SIMMERED HIJIKI
2 tablespoons (5 g) dried hijiki
1 tablespoon soy sauce
1 tablespoon mirin
1 tablespoon sake
1 tablespoon sugar

For the simmered hijiki, place the hijiki in a large bowl, cover with some just-boiled water and leave for 30 minutes to rehydrate fully. Drain and rinse well. If you are using the stem of the plant rather than the sprouts, you might need to roughly chop them.

Place the rehydrated hijiki in a small saucepan with the soy sauce, mirin, sake and sugar. Bring to a gentle simmer over low heat and cook for about 10 minutes until well reduced.

Mix the simmered hijiki together with the rice until evenly distributed. Divide into 6 portions and wet your hands. Dip the tip of your finger in some salt and rub it between your hands. Shape each rice portion into a cylinder, lightly pressing it into shape, and using wet, salty hands each time.

Cut the nori into 6 strips and wrap them around the cylinders. If you aren't eating these immediately – for example, if you're putting them in a bento box – keep the cut nori separate from the rice, perhaps in a resealable bag. Once you've wrapped them with nori, enjoy immediately.

Continued ›

第五の味覚、うま味

The science behind umami, our fifth taste

To understand how kombu dashi is a secret ingredient and why you should use it, you need only hear the story of Kikunae Ikeda, a professor of chemistry at Tokyo Imperial University and the man who discovered umami over a century ago.

Ikeda was enjoying his wife's kombu soup one night – it was even more tasty than usual – and his thoughts turned to the potential of kombu to impart flavour to a dish. This led him down a rabbit hole of working out how to capture that flavour. One year later, in 1908, he managed to isolate 30 grams (1 ounce) of crystals of glutamate – the amino acids that are one of the main components of umami – simmered down from a hefty 12 kilograms (26 pounds) of kombu dashi, to create monosodium glutamate (MSG). He packaged it as *ajinomoto* ('essence of flavour') to sell to housewives to be used to enhance their everyday cooking.

He also coined the term umami (旨味, which comes from *umai*, delicious, and *mi*, taste), to explain the flavour of kombu and other ingredients that didn't fit into the four 'tastes' – sweet, sour, bitter, salty – that were already established. He proposed umami as our fifth taste. Ikeda noticed other foods that, along with kombu, fit this category but not the others, such as mushrooms (particularly dried), fermented fish, green tea and asparagus. Today, we know that Parmesan cheese and ketchup (in fact, all tomatoes) are also umami rich.

What exactly does umami taste like? According to Tokyo's Umami Information Centre, it's a mild and delicate flavour, yet it fills the mouth and is exceptionally long lasting and lingering, compared to other tastes. It is also, quite literally, mouth-watering: it stimulates saliva production, making us more readily able to swallow food and more receptive to flavours.

To explain it simply, the presence of umami signifies the presence of proteins. When these proteins break down, amino acids are created; and each different type of amino acid can have a different taste – salty, sweet, sour, bitter or umami. The more protein, the more amino acids, so potentially, the more flavour/umami. Umami is made up of three components: the amino acid glutamate, which can be found in a wide variety of foods; inosinate, which is mainly found in animal-based foods such as meat and fish; and guanylate, which can be found in dried mushrooms.

Interestingly, the process of fermentation can increase the amount of umami in a food. This is the case with fermented foods from all over the world, from soy sauce to Vietnamese or Thai fish sauce, to cured meats and cheeses such as prosciutto and Parmigiano. In the process of curing meats, the volume of glutamate can increase by 50 times; while, in cheese, glutamate is created over time so the longer the cheese ages, the more umami is present.

So, these fermented ingredients our ancestors learned to create and enjoy over hundreds of years, not only had a practical purpose of preserving food, but they were also delicious and full of nutrients to guarantee our survival.

We, as humans, seem to be naturally drawn to umami; we adore it. It is no coincidence that the very first food many of us taste, breastmilk, is rich in it. Even those who weren't raised on breastmilk would have become familiar with this flavour before birth – it is present in amniotic fluid. Scientists, thanks to Ikeda, now realise that umami signals to the brain that proteins are present – telling us not only that a food is safe to eat (in the same way bitterness can signal a potentially harmful food), but also that this food contains an essential nutrient for our survival. Recent studies have also shown that umami detected in the stomach sends another signal to the body to digest and absorb the protein. Our bodies are designed to want and need umami.

There is also something peculiar and powerful that umami does when it comes into contact with other ingredients: it boosts all the other flavours in the dish, enhancing the taste of individual ingredients *up to eight times*. Think about how a spoonful of Parmesan in minestrone or on a pasta dish transforms that dish. This is how kombu dashi can be your ultimate secret ingredient, uplifting every dish it goes into, adding a deep and intense savouriness to sauces, miso soup, noodle soup and stews. I often use it in place of water, even when I only need a splash.

So, not only does umami tell our bodies, '*Hey, there is protein here that you need*' and then helps our bodies absorb it, but it also makes everything we're eating with it taste great. ●

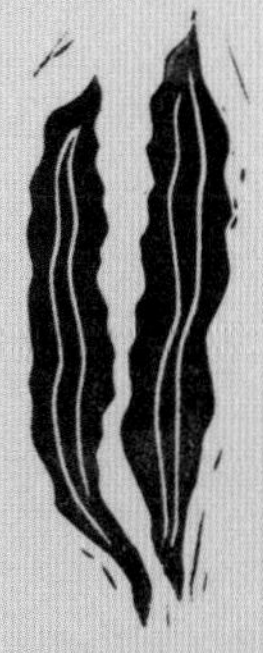

炊き込みご飯

HIJIKI & MACKEREL RICE

TAKIKOMI GOHAN

Takikomi gohan is one of my favourite things – for me, this is the ultimate one-pot meal. You just layer everything together in a pot or rice cooker, put a lid on and let it all steam together until it's done. The layering is important because the rice needs to be undisturbed so it cooks evenly underneath. This is also very adaptable; you can tweak it to your tastes or what you have around you.

Hijiki seaweed is the star of this recipe: I love that you only need a little and can just reach for it in the pantry. It has such a wonderful aroma and earthy flavour that reminds me of mushrooms. I once read a description that it smells 'like a forest after a rain shower', and I couldn't agree more.

VARIATIONS: The variations are endless but, to narrow things down, you could use diced raw chicken thigh meat, or tinned tuna instead of mackerel (or leave it out). Often aburaage (fried tofu) is paired with hijiki – it is a great source of protein and is wonderful for soaking up the sauce that seasons this dish. You could add dried shiitake mushrooms, or perhaps edamame for more colour, or just some chopped spring onions. Play it by ear.

SERVES 4

2 tablespoons (5 g) dried hijiki
300 g (10 oz) Japanese rice
340 ml (1⅓ cups) water (or kombu dashi, page 108)
1 tablespoon soy sauce
1 tablespoon mirin
1 tablespoon sake
½ carrot, peeled and cut into matchsticks
100 g (3½ oz) lotus root, thinly sliced and cut into halves or quarters
100 g (3½ oz) tinned mackerel, drained

Place the hijiki in a bowl, cover with some just-boiled water and leave for 30 minutes to rehydrate fully. Drain and rinse well.

Wash the rice and drain – do this a few times until the water is not so cloudy. Place the rice in a saucepan (or rice cooker) and add the measured water or dashi, soy sauce, mirin and sake. Scatter the vegetables, mackerel and, finally, the hijiki over the top. Don't be tempted to mix this; it's important the layers are undisturbed so the rice cooks evenly.

Bring to a simmer over low–medium heat, then immediately put on the lid and reduce to the lowest heat. Cook for 15 minutes and check a rice grain to see if it is soft. If it's ready, let it continue steaming, covered and off the heat, for a further 10–15 minutes. If using a rice cooker, simply select the normal setting for cooking rice.

Finally, you can mix the rice. Use a spatula to mix gently, so you don't squash the grains. Serve straightaway in bowls. This also makes excellent onigiri (page 121).

ひじきサラダ

HIJIKI SALAD

This is all about the hijiki dressing, which is inspired by one made in the charming Maruya Cafe on Shimo-kamagari Island in the middle of the Seto Inland Sea. The owner, Anna Hamashita, produces a range of her cafe's most popular dressings with local ingredients: hijiki, and citrus fruits such as sudachi and daidai, together with her uncle's locally grown olive oil.

VARIATIONS: Like any salad, you can and should make this your own, using what you have to hand. Some other things that would go well here include julienned carrot, poached chicken, thinly sliced daikon, blanched snow peas (mangetout) or green beans, diced tofu, cherry tomatoes or avocado. Also, try the dressing on chilled tofu, steamed vegetables, even grilled fish or chicken.

SERVES 2–4 as part of a meal

50 g (2 cups) small salad leaves such as baby spinach or rocket
⅓ long cucumber, halved lengthways and finely sliced
5 radishes, finely sliced
¼ red onion, finely sliced
½ teaspoon sesame seeds

DRESSING

2 tablespoons rehydrated hijiki, chopped (see note)
1 tablespoon soy sauce
1 tablespoon rice vinegar
pinch of sugar
1 teaspoon sesame or olive oil

Arrange the salad leaves, cucumber, radish and onion on a platter.

Mix together the dressing ingredients to dissolve the sugar, which gives a nice balance to this. Taste to see if you need to adjust anything, then pour over the salad and toss well. Sprinkle with sesame seeds.

Note: You only need a very tiny quantity of hijiki here to get 2 tablespoons when it is rehydrated – just a small pinch, as it expands to about 10 times its size. Put it in a bowl, cover with water and leave for 30 minutes until it has rehydrated.

抹茶寒天ゼリー

MATCHA KANTEN JELLY

Kanten makes a wonderful firm, refreshing jelly that is quick to set (it sets at room temperature too) and easy to customise with any flavour you like. I love the colour and flavour of matcha in desserts; for me, it goes hand in hand with my absolute favourite Japanese sweet, anko, or red bean paste. If you don't have anko, you could leave it out or replace it with some good vanilla ice cream.

This is a kind of simplified anmitsu – an old-fashioned dessert from Tokyo's fashionable Ginza neighbourhood. Anmitsu has many variations, but usually has some combination of mame (boiled sweet mame peas), colourful fruit, dango (mochi balls), cubes of kanten jelly, anko, ice cream and kuromitsu (black sugar syrup).

So, feel free to customise this to your liking with the variations below. I sometimes find a full anmitsu is too much – this daintier version is just the thing to have with a cup of tea.

VARIATIONS: Add slices of fresh fruit – strawberries or mandarin segments are very pretty with matcha-coloured desserts. Add a couple of dango (page 259). Try another tea for the jelly – earthy, roasted hojicha powder is also wonderful, or try earl grey tea – or just leave them plain (with a touch of sugar). Use vanilla (or black sesame or matcha) ice cream instead of anko; and maple syrup or sweetened condensed milk in place of kuromitsu (as I've done in the picture here).

SERVES 4

MATCHA JELLY

- 2 teaspoons premium matcha powder
- 250 ml (1 cup) water
- 2 teaspoons sugar
- 2 teaspoons kanten

KUROMITSU SYRUP

- 2 tablespoons black Okinawan sugar or brown sugar
- 1 tablespoon water

TO SERVE

- 200 g (7 oz) anko (page 256)
- 2 teaspoons kinako powder

To make the jelly, dissolve the matcha in a little of the water first to make a paste – I do this directly in a small pan. Slowly add the rest of the water, then the sugar and kanten. Bring to a simmer and cook for 1–2 minutes over medium heat. Pour into an ice cube tray (or use a 20 x 10 cm/8 x 4 in baking tin and cut into cubes when set). Leave to cool – it should set at room temperature. To get the cubes out of the tray, run a knife down one side – they should turn out fairly easily.

For the kuromitsu syrup, heat the sugar and water together for 2 minutes or until dissolved and slightly thickened.

To put the dessert together, divide the anko into 4 portions and squeeze each one in your hand so it takes on the indentations of your fingers. Place in a bowl with about 5 cubes of matcha jelly. Add a little of the kuromitsu syrup (or maple syrup or condensed milk) and dust with kinako to serve.

日本酒
SAKE

真澄
MASUMI
真澄
MASUMI
真澄
MASUMI

日本酒
SAKE

'Sake is the best medicine of all.'

JAPANESE PROVERB

Sake, or nihonshu, which was added to UNESCO's Intangible Cultural Heritage list in 2024, is often described as 'rice wine' in English. However, rather than a simple fermentation like wine, the way sake is made is more like beer – it is brewed from polished rice with the help of koji mould. Koji gives the rice enzymes that break down the starch molecules into sugar, which are then converted to alcohol. Over a series of different fermentations, sake is made.

It might be Japan's national beverage but, today, there are only around 1200 breweries producing sake. Even in the aftermath of the Second World War there were around 4000 breweries in Japan and just over a century ago there were 30,000. This number is surprising to me – I can't help comparing it to Italy, where there are over 250,000 winemakers. Japanese sake brewing is in sharp decline because the request for sake has waned, while other national beverages, including shochu, have become more popular.

This isn't a new phenomenon: it has been happening slowly over the past 50 years; sake consumption in Japan has declined by 76 per cent since the 1970s. In 1978 the *Washington Post* published an article on the rising popularity of beer and whisky in Japan. Internationally, however, the interest in sake has increased and, as a result, the Japanese government has recently lifted some regulations on opening new kura (sake breweries) if the sake is to be exported. It would be a great loss if sake brewing became a dying art.

Sake is inextricably linked to Japanese culture and, in particular, the cuisine, where it is not only for drinking alongside meals, but is vital in cooking typical Japanese dishes. Sake lends a subtle and elegant umami flavour, and is excellent for tenderising meat and also for removing unwanted strong odours from meat and fish – they evaporate along with the alcohol during cooking.

Because of sake's utterly unique flavour and aroma, I would go so far as to say that it is an irreplaceable ingredient in Japanese cooking. You simply cannot substitute another ingredient for sake; there is nothing that will do what sake does in these dishes.

The sake process starts every autumn with the steaming of new-season rice. About a quarter of the rice is inoculated with koji. A yeast starter (called moto) is then made with the koji-inoculated rice, steamed rice, water and a selected yeast – the important role of the yeast here is to make sure that if a rogue yeast or bacteria gets in, it won't be able to take over because of the abundance of the selected yeast. More rice and water is then added, three times, to this yeasty mash (called moromi). It is left to ferment for 20–40 days, then pressed and filtered. The sake that is filtered is then usually pasteurised, left to mature for about six months, filtered again, and then finally bottled.

The solids left over from the pressing are called *kasu*, sake lees (see page 138). These are also used in the kitchen for pickling and, more creatively, baking.

As you might imagine, one of the most important ingredients in sake-making is rice. Rice for sake is different from rice for cooking – premium sake is made with sake rice, but it is not a given for the rest. Sake rice is much more expensive, for starters. It is a taller, larger plant with larger grains and more starch, which is concentrated right in the middle of the grain so that, when it is polished, only the desired starch in the centre of the grain remains. Cooking rice has more fat and protein than starch, and they are all mixed together within the grain.

Many sake breweries faced a shortage of sake rice during the Covid pandemic. With restaurants closed, fewer people were drinking sake and rice farmers couldn't sell their sake rice. During the following uncertain seasons, many farmers didn't bother growing sake rice, since they couldn't sell it. Still now, years later, there is a shortage of sake rice because many farmers haven't returned to growing it.

Renowned sake expert John Gauntner writes about these current challenges to sake production in his newsletter, *Sake Industry News*: 'When there is a bad harvest of wine grapes, winemakers don't really look over the fence and start making wine with grapes normally used for making raisins… In Japan, however, rice is everything. And many sake breweries *do* use table rice for their sake. There *is* crossover and, in the event of a tug of war over rice stocks between sake breweries and restaurants and Japanese households, you can be sure the sake industry would lose. Nihonshu is important to Japanese culture and its people, but not more important than rice.'

The milling and polishing of the rice is another important factor in the making of sake – the more the rice is milled, the better the sake quality. To give you an idea of the importance of this: top sakes have 50 per cent or less of the rice grain remaining after milling, while table sake might have 70 per cent of the rice remaining.

Perhaps the most important feature of a good sake is that it has been handmade with care. As John Gauntner describes: 'Each step of the sake-making process becomes the foundation for the next, and the success of any step depends hugely on all that has come before it. So, quality resulting from painstaking effort early on is carried through to the end. How the rice is washed, soaked and steamed affects the koji making, which in turn affects the fermentation, and this chain continues until the product is complete.'

At my favourite artisanal sake brewery, Terada Honke, not far from my mother's hometown in Chiba, they not only make everything by hand, using traditional materials and tools such as kioke wooden barrels, but, as the moromi is being stirred, the toji (the master brewer) and workers sing in unison, sending good vibrations to the sake.

Sake-making as we know it today has a history of well over 1000 years in Japan, but the beginnings of sake brewing can be traced to the second century BC, when the knowledge of fermenting rice into alcohol arrived from China. By 715, there is the first record of sake brewing with koji by the Imperial Court. But perhaps one of the most important periods was between the 12th and 14th centuries, when sake was introduced to Shinto temples, where they began producing it – the ritual and the drink became intertwined with Shintoism as a connection between mortals and the gods. Premium sake, meanwhile, has only been around since the 1980s.

Sake is more than just a drink in Japan: it is part of the most important cultural festivities. In Japanese weddings, for example, there is a special sake ceremony called *sansankudo*, 三三九度, (literally: 'three times three, nine times'). The bride and groom take turns sipping three times from three special sake cups to seal their bond. (My mother hand-carried her family's set of sake cups from Japan to Italy so that we could do this at my wedding.)

Likewise, sharing sake in any situation in Japanese culture is a broader symbol of a bond at the start of a new relationship, job, venture or community. And it is the way we begin every new year, with a wish for good health and a cup of otoso (page 166).

TYPES OF SAKE

The most common sake, table sake (**futsushu**), makes up the biggest part of the market. This kind of sake is cut with distilled alcohol – a practice left over from the Second World War when there were severe rice shortages. The government enforced this practice so more sake could be produced while using fewer precious rice resources; this volume-enhancing method has remained normal practice ever since. Not until 1964 did any breweries go back to the traditional rice-only sake brewing; today only about 10 per cent of sake, known as **junmai**, is made in this way.

The top four grades of sake, also known collectively as 'premium sake', are called **ginjo**: **junmai ginjo**, **ginjo**, **junmai daiginjo** and **daiginjo.**

Regular ginjo and daiginjo also have some, strictly limited, amounts of alcohol added to them, although for other reasons: to bring out the aromas; to adjust the alcohol content during the sake-making process (always around 16 per cent); and for stability.

With junmai sake (junmai ginjo and junmai daiginjo), you can be sure there is no added alcohol: only rice, water and koji.

There are also other types of sake that don't fit into these categories, for example, **nigorizake** and **namazake**, cloudy sake or unpasteurised sake. There is also a small amount of **aged sake** and, while quite a different product, there is **sparkling sake** too. It should be noted that, while none of these would be good for cooking with, they are certainly enjoyable and fun to explore to accompany food (I personally love cloudy sake, warm or chilled). Cheap **cooking sake** is usually sold in small plastic bottles and is perfectly fine for cooking with. It will add a delicately sweet, umami flavour to dishes and even tenderises meat.

HOW TO STORE SAKE

Unlike wine, sake should not be stored and aged, but should be enjoyed right away, while young and definitely within the year. New-season sake is made over the winter, using the autumn's new-harvest rice, for the new year. To store it, keep it cool and out of the sunlight. If you have room in the fridge, it will keep well there until you are ready to drink it. Once opened, it should keep for up to a week, although if you're using it only for cooking you should be fine to keep it much longer.

HOW TO SERVE SAKE

Sake is traditionally served out of a small carafe (tokkuri) in little cups called ochoko. You might be served sake in a little wooden box called a masu with a glass in it. The sake gets poured into the glass until it overflows in the box. My personal favourite tradition when ordering sake is choosing your own cup from a tray full of completely different cups – ceramic, glass, wood, all unique colours and sizes, many handmade with imperfections. You pick the cup that speaks to you. I like to do this when serving sake to my guests too. The main thing to remember is that the glass or cup does not affect sake as it would wine, so serve sake in anything you like.

Sake can be served chilled, warm or at room temperature. As a general guide, ginjo might be served chilled and junmai warm. But this can also depend on the season, the weather, how you are feeling or what you're eating with it. Five hundred years ago, all sake was always served warm, as the Florentine merchant Francesco Carletti recounts from his travels in 1597–98: 'They always drink the wine hot, whether in summer or in winter, taking it in small sips and enjoying it much more than we enjoy drinking a bowl of broth.'

Warming a sake can bring out the umami and sweetness. To warm sake, make a hot water bath: heat a pot of water to 50°C (122°F) and place the sake in a vessel (for example, a ceramic vase or pot) in the pot. The water should come up well past halfway. Keep it here until the sake reaches at least 40°C (104°F) – this should take a few minutes, depending on the vessel. You can also warm sake in the microwave – again, be gentle; you don't want to cook it or make it too hot.

There is some etiquette to serving sake in formal settings in Japan. A good first rule to remember is that you should never refill your own cup, but you should fill everyone else's cup. Whether you're receiving or pouring the sake, always hold the cup or tokkuri with both hands. And if you don't want to drink any more sake, don't finish your cup – an empty cup will always be refilled. (My husband learned this the hard way on his first trip to Japan!) In a casual setting, though, you can relax and not worry too much about these formalities and just enjoy the sake.

What is sake lees?

Sake lees, or kasu (酒粕 or さけかす) in Japanese, is left over from the sake-making process. Once the fermentation has finished and the sake is pressed, the kasu is the remaining mash that is eventually discarded. But the traditional concept of mottainai (the feeling of regret when something of value is wasted) is strongly ingrained in Japan and so kasu can be easily found in shops, online and directly from sake breweries.

No sake kasu is like another – every brewery uses different percentages and varieties of rice, different yeasts, different fermenting processes and different machines and methods of pressing the sake. You will find sake lees in many different forms and flavours, which, in turn, affects how you use it in recipes.

If you find sake kasu that is made from premium sakes, such as junmai daiginjo, junmai ginjo, daiginjo and ginjo (which would usually be written on the packet), these tend to be more fruity and also more fluid as they have been pressed less. If you're using a regular sake lees (which probably won't have the type of sake written on it), it might be less fragrant and have a firmer consistency. There is even a mirin kasu, which is naturally very sweet and glutinous because of the glutinous rice used for mirin-making.

Confusingly, sake lees also comes in a variety of different forms, resulting from the particular process of each brewery. There is a paste form, known as nerikasu (this could be on the runnier, softer side or quite thick and firm, see photo on the left) and there is an aged version of nerikasu that has the colour and texture of miso (this one is sweet and richly flavoured, great for pickles, see photo on the right). Or it can take the form of a firm sheet known as itakasu (this needs to be soaked in warm water), a crumbly version of itakasu (barakasu), or even a powder (simply dehydrated lees that has been finely ground).

For the recipes in this book, I would choose the paste form: nerikasu.

Sake lees has very interesting health benefits – it's high in protein and vitamin B, and is useful for digestion and lowering blood pressure and cholesterol, among other things. As an ingredient, it can add complex flavours and umami to dishes. Add it to soup, mix with miso as a marinade, use it to make fluffy bread or cakes, or even in homemade ice cream.

It is usually slightly alcoholic (around six to eight per cent), so be aware of this if you're not cooking it completely. On the other hand, the alcohol content makes sake lees very long lasting, so, if you manage to find some, you can keep it in the fridge and take your time trying out recipes, such as the sake lees pickles (page 144), cheesecake (page 160) and amazake (page 162).

MIRIN みりん

I believe mirin is often misunderstood; perhaps because it is seen as a condiment, rather than an alcoholic drink in its own right with a 500-year history, and also because there are many kinds of 'mirin' on offer and the one that usually makes it out of Japan is not actually mirin but a mirin-alternative that you could say is nothing more than syrup.

Real mirin, which is called *hon-mirin* (本みりん), where hon means 'real', is a rice wine similar to sake, but it is made with a different kind of rice – glutinous rice – and contains added shochu, a distilled alcoholic drink (usually 25 per cent alcohol) that can be made from a range of ingredients, including rice, sweet potatoes, buckwheat and brown sugar.

Like sake, hon-mirin begins with steamed rice and koji. To this, shochu is added to make a moromi mash that will mature in tanks for about two months in a process of saccharification. During this time, the rice mash is broken down into saccharides and amino acids by the koji enzymes, but the presence of shochu prevents fermentation of the mash, which would remove the sugar – this is how mirin gets its sweet umami flavour. The liquid is then squeezed out of the mash and the mirin is matured for a year before being bottled.

During the Edo period, mirin was consumed only as a drink, as a kind of sweet sake. Today it is almost only used in cooking, where it adds richness, shine and that unique flavour that is both sweet and umami. Often, however, what is used is not actually mirin, but one of the syrupy mirin-alternatives.

Why is this the case? After the Second World War Japan faced a national rice shortage and so, similar to the restrictions in sake- and vinegar-making, the production of mirin was temporarily banned, lifting only after eight years. During this time an imitation mirin was developed. It was simple, cheap, it had no alcohol, but it was also not at all related to real mirin, hence the use of the term *hon-mirin*, literally 'real mirin', to distinguish traditional mirin from this alternative.

However, during those eight years, the cheaper, simpler mirin took hold as a preferred ingredient in the market. The fact that it doesn't contain alcohol meant it could be sold in places that didn't have an alcohol licence. This is still the case – you will only find hon-mirin in places that are allowed to sell alcohol, thanks to the presence of shochu in its making.

WHAT MIRIN TO LOOK FOR

If you live outside Japan, 'fake mirin' might be the only one you have ever seen on the market. It is basically a syrup. You might find different grades of this cheaper mirin: there is one that has no alcohol or almost no alcohol, but has some salt. You can also find one that is made with sake instead of shochu and has a slightly lower alcohol content than hon-mirin. This might also contain glucose or corn syrup.

Aji-mirin is a mirin condiment and is quite a different thing again. Aji means 'taste', so it 'tastes like mirin' but is made with salt, syrup, glucose, alcohol and rice and has an alcohol content of around eight to 14 per cent.

Hon-mirin, the real thing

Living abroad, I've noticed that it is a lot easier to buy the simpler, glucose-based mirin. To be honest, I don't think there is anything wrong in using it if you cannot find hon-mirin; but, if you do have a choice, here are some reasons why you should go for the real thing.

Real mirin contains alcohol, similarly to wine, usually around 14 per cent. This alcohol content is one of the superpowers of mirin. Like sake, mirin is often used in Japanese cooking to remove strong odours, particularly of meat and fish – the odours evaporate along with the alcohol during cooking.

Mirin also helps vegetables such as potatoes hold their shape during cooking – alcohol suppresses the dissolving of pectin in cell walls. Mirin does this better than just any alcohol, as described here by Takashi Sato, an eighth-generation tamari soy sauce producer behind San-J in Virginia, USA: 'So, all we need is alcohol? The answer is no. The other original characteristics of mirin – saccharides and low pH – prevent the pectin from being dissolved.'

Hon-mirin also has a very balanced sweetness and umami flavour that is more subtle than the mirin alternatives. So, if you do have the chance, this is the one you want.

A NOTE ON MIRIN SUBSTITUTES

If you don't have mirin, in its place you could use sake with a bit of sugar. If you don't have sake, you could just add some sugar (my preference is demerara sugar, which is less sweet but has a bit more of a caramel flavour) or honey. While the sugar replaces mirin's sweetness, be aware that it won't be quite the same, as both mirin and sake have properties that tenderise meat, for example, or add umami.

I wouldn't recommend trying anything else – I have heard suggestions of vinegar, white wine or dessert wine, Chinese Shaoxing wine, but these would totally alter the delicately balanced flavours required, so please avoid them at all cost.

煎り酒

SAKE & UMEBOSHI DRESSING

IRIZAKE

I found this recipe for irizake (literally meaning 'roasted sake') while looking through a 17th century cookbook and it stopped me in my tracks: 'Mix one sho [an ancient form of measurement that would be equivalent to 1.8 litres/61 fl oz] katsuobushi with 15–20 umeboshi. Add two sho of aged sake, a little water and a little tamari. Boil down to one sho and let cool.' What a umami bomb!

This came from *Ryori Monogatari* (料理物語), one of the earliest Japanese cookbooks, published by an anonymous author in 1643. At this time, the Edo period, Japan had finally been unified after over a century of civil war. The nation, fearing colonialism, isolated itself from the outside world, but this was also a period of general peace, when not only did Japanese food become more refined and defined, but also literary works, such as this cookbook, history books and travel journals detailing local delicacies, were made.

The author of the *Ryori Monogatari* describes the intention of the book as documenting recipes from oral traditions that have been passed down and collected from people all over the country. It has been translated from the original, which is held in Tokyo's Metropolitan Library, into English by Joshua L Badgley, who has generously created a free website for anyone who would like to read through it.

When I looked into irizake, I realised why I had not heard much about it. It was popular during the Edo period but then seems to have disappeared until the Second World War when, during shortages of soy sauce (among many things), people turned to making irizake at home and using it as they would soy sauce. Once supplies of soy sauce returned, irizake seems to have been forgotten again but is now making a comeback in high-end Japanese restaurants, particularly for pairing with sashimi. It is an incredible seasoning, full of flavour, that also works well as a dressing for fish or chicken, any vegetables or salads. I tasted some wonderful daikon pickles at the beautiful Masumi brewery shop in Nagano, where they used irizake to flavour the pickles.

If you want to try something similar, use 2 tablespoons of this irizake, 1 tablespoon vinegar and 2 teaspoons sugar to pickle a thinly sliced 5 cm (2 in) piece of daikon and a julienned 5 cm (2 in) piece of ginger.

Don't use a cooking sake for this, but you also don't need to use an expensive bottle – just a simple bottle of sake will do.

VARIATIONS: Vegetarians can leave out the katsuobushi. There is actually a specific vegetarian version of irizake in the *Ryori Monogatari* that includes tofu and dried turnip in place of the katsuobushi. I think you could use dried shiitake mushrooms or kombu, too.

MAKES 170 ml (⅔ cup)

375 ml (1½ cups) sake
185 ml (¾ cup) water
2 umeboshi plums
5 g (½ cup) katsuobushi flakes

Place the sake, water and umeboshi in a saucepan and bring to a lively simmer over medium–high heat. Simmer until the liquid has reduced by half; this can take about 15 minutes but keep an eye on it – all pans and heat sources are different.

Add the katsuobushi, turn off the heat and leave to steep for about 10 minutes. Strain the liquid back into the pan and reduce further, to your liking.

You should end up with about one third the liquid you started with, but, oh, will it be delicious! If you have a very special artisanal soy sauce, you could add a drop of this as well. Keep in a jar in the fridge and use within the week.

粕漬け

SAKE LEES PICKLES

KASUZUKE

Vegetables pickled in the leftover lees after sake-making have a long history in Japan. Narazuke, sake-pickled white melon, is said to be one of the first pickles mentioned in documents dating to almost 1300 years ago. You can find packaged sake lees all year round but, if you happen to be visiting Japan (or know any sake-makers) over the winter season, when sake-making is in full swing, keep your eye out for it.

In the town of Saijo in Ehime prefecture, at a 130-year-old family-run sake brewery called Seiryo, we met Shizue-san, the sake brewer's mother, who showed us her impressive collection of kasuzuke barrels where she pickles vegetables in three-year-old sake lees. It was a revelation – her aged sake lees had become a deep amber colour, like miso, and it gave the vegetables a caramel-like flavour. We tasted local seasonal vegetables such as fuki (butterbur, a long-stemmed plant that is crunchy like celery), bamboo shoots and cucumber, together with her family's sake – a wonderful match.

As sake kasu is so variable, the flavour and fragrance changes according to the type of sake and brewing process. I suggest playing around with the proportions slightly here. If using a premium ginjo sake lees, which can be fruity and aromatic, you might prefer a bit more miso, or a stronger-flavoured miso, or to use less sugar, for example. It is all about balance. Dip your finger in and have a taste before adjusting to your liking. Try any vegetables you like here; my preference is for root vegetables – daikon, carrots, turnips – over more watery vegetables such as cucumbers.

You can eat these after a day, or age them for as long as you like. It's difficult for them to go bad because of the slightly alcoholic environment of the sake lees, but they will age and change, the flavour will get stronger, perhaps funkier, and the vegetables will lose water and become less crunchy. You will find a moment when these pickles are ideal for you – mine is when they are fresher, one or two days in.

MAKES 1 small jar

2 carrots, or similar, peeled
100 g (⅓ cup) sake lees
1 tablespoon white miso
1 tablespoon raw (demerara) sugar
pinch of salt

Cut the carrots on the diagonal about 1 cm (½ in) thick.

Combine the sake lees, miso, sugar and salt in a bowl. If using a very firm lees, you can add a splash of water to loosen the paste, but just know that water will be drawn out of the vegetables too.

Add the carrots, turning them in the paste so they are well coated. Pickle them overnight and try them the next day – rinse or just wipe off the excess sake lees. You can keep pickling for several days – or even age them!

Note: In the spirit of mottainai, don't throw away the sake lees after pickling. You can re-use the paste for pickling a second or third time, or try adding it to miso soup.

お雑煮

NEW YEAR'S SOUP

OZONI

This is one of the classic dishes eaten in Japan for the New Year's meal, which is known as osechi ryori (page 149). Ozoni has a couple of regional variations. In the Kansai region (the south of Honshu, around the old capital Kyoto) it is usually a white miso soup with vegetables and traditional round mochi; whereas in Kanto region (Tokyo and eastern Japan) it is a clear soup with chicken and rectangular mochi cakes. Sake plays an important role in delicate clear soups, adding an elegant note of umami.

Naturally, each household has a favourite way to prepare this soup. As I live outside Japan, getting some of the traditional ingredients – such as taro, kamaboko (fish cakes) or strips of yuzu – is a challenge, so I usually make it with these easier-to-find ingredients.

Dried mochi blocks are easy to find now; they are shelf stable and long lasting and I always have them in my pantry. All you need to do is grill or toast them on a hot pan until they become very soft and chewy inside. They are scored, so it's easy to break them into two or four pieces with your hands – it is bad luck to cut mochi with a knife, so don't get off on the wrong foot at the beginning of the year! And be careful when eating mochi: they are deceptively hot and chewy and should be eaten carefully, so as not to choke when you bite into them.

Ozoni can be served in lacquered miso soup bowls and eaten for breakfast, the first meal of the new year, after a sip of otoso, the special herb-infused sake (page 166).

VARIATION: Vegetarians can simply leave out the chicken (or add taro, if you have it).

SERVES 2

1 mochi block, broken in half
1 boneless chicken thigh, diced
2 tablespoons sake
pinch of salt
2 shiitake mushrooms
2 stalks English spinach (or 1 handful of baby spinach)
4 carrot slices
4 daikon slices, halved or quartered
250 ml (1 cup) dashi (pages 108–9)
1 teaspoon usukuchi soy sauce

Break the mochi in half and toast on a hot dry frying pan for about 3 minutes each side, until puffed and crisp and with some dark brown marks.

Marinate the chicken in half the sake and a pinch of salt while you prepare the vegetables. If using dried shiitake mushrooms, rehydrate them first in warm water and then cut off the stems.

The spinach should be washed and blanched. If using English spinach, cut into 3–4 cm (1½ in) pieces after blanching. Some people like to carve the carrot and daikon slices into pretty shapes.

Make the dashi and add the daikon and carrot. Simmer for about 5 minutes, then add the soy sauce and the rest of the sake, the shiitake and the chicken. Cook for 10 minutes, or until the daikon and carrot are tender.

Pour into bowls, adding spinach to each bowl and topping with the mochi. Enjoy straightaway.

おせち料理

Osechi ryori

Osechi ryori refers to the New Year's meal, arguably the most important meal of the entire year. Unlike most of the rest of Asia, Japan doesn't celebrate the Lunar New Year and, naturally, Christmas is not officially celebrated either. So, this is the one very special time of the year to celebrate with family and it takes place on the first of January.

Rather than festive, the mood for New Year is decidedly more serious than in other countries, but one way it is celebrated is with special symbolic foods – the first meal of the year is to bring the family good health, abundance and good fortune.

Some of the typical foods include ozoni soup (page 146); datemaki, a sweet rolled omelette; kamaboko, which is a red and white fish cake (auspicious because the colours are those of the Japanese flag); namasu (a rice vinegar pickle with matchsticks of carrot and daikon); and herring roe or kazunoko, which symbolises having many children. Kuromame, or black soybeans (page 252), is one of my favourites. Prawns cooked in sake and soy sauce is another important dish: the bent shape of the prawns recalls the hunched posture of an elderly person, symbolising long life.

All these foods can be eaten cold, so they are prepared with love and care over the days leading up to New Year and arranged in pretty lacquered boxes. You can also share otoso (page 166), sake infused with a special selection of medicinal herbs that will bring good health to the family and even, as tradition has it, the entire village. ●

帆立てのムニエル

SCALLOPS COOKED IN BUTTER & SAKE

HOTATE NO MUNIERU

Scallops, or hotate (ほたて), are much loved in Japan and are often eaten raw (my favourite sashimi). But seared with butter and sake they are absolutely divine.

This cooking style is called 'munieru' in Japanese, adopted from the French, *meunière*, which means 'miller style'. It is used to describe a dish of any fish or meat dusted in flour (as the miller would have dusted things in flour, naturally) and cooked in butter. What is noticeably absent in this recipe is the flour – simply because you do not need it. The scallops cook so quickly, getting that wonderful caramelised sear, that you might burn the flour. So, forget the flour and, instead, deglaze the pan with sake. Add the butter at the end so it doesn't burn.

You can serve this on its own as a starter, or keep it for two and make a lunch out of it with miso soup and steamed rice topped with some strips of nori.

VARIATIONS: You could replace the scallops with king prawns in their shells. You can cook mussels similarly: you'll need a pan with deep sides and, instead of trying to sear the mussels, you want to steam them open, so pour in the sake and then cover with a lid and toss them about for 2–3 minutes. When they've all (or mostly all) opened, add the cold butter and toss to coat everything.

SERVES 2–4

12 fresh scallops
pinch of salt
60 ml (¼) cup sake
40 g (1½ oz) cold butter

Pat the scallops dry and season with salt. Heat a frying pan over high heat and, when very hot, sear the scallops for about 60–90 seconds on each side. Pour in the sake.

After a minute, turn off the heat and add the butter, using this melted buttery sauce to baste the scallops.

Serve immediately.

とりの梅煮

UMEBOSHI-BRAISED CHICKEN

TORI NO UMENI

Umeboshi (梅干し) are unripe Japanese plums that have been salt-pickled and sun-dried. Even though ume are green when picked, umeboshi is usually red because reddish-purple shiso leaves are one of the traditional additions to pickled plums. They are eye-wateringly sour and salty, which might surprise you the first time; but then, I think, you easily become enamoured of them and cannot live without them.

Umeboshi are beloved in Japan by adults and children alike and are found in the most everyday of dishes: from inside onigiri or on top of rice in bento boxes; for breakfast or on ochazuke (page 246). In fact, there is an equivalent expression for 'an apple a day keeps the doctor away', but with umeboshi in Japan, because these are an important health food, helping aid digestion and ward off fatigue.

If you too are an umeboshi lover (or are trying to become one), this homely one-pot dish is for you. It is a deceptive recipe because there are so few ingredients, but the combination of sour umeboshi, umami from the sake, and a bit of sugar and ginger creates an irresistible sweet and sour sauce that is full of flavour.

VARIATION: Vegans, try this with thick slices of eggplant (aubergine) or whole baby eggplants.

SERVES 4

4 boneless chicken thighs, skin on (about 600 g/1 lb 5 oz)
vegetable oil for the pan
60 ml (¼ cup) sake
4 umeboshi
1 tablespoon raw (demerara) sugar
1 teaspoon grated ginger
steamed rice (page 36), to serve

Make some incisions along the skin side of the chicken to help it cook evenly. Sear the chicken, first skin-side-down, in a lightly oiled casserole dish over high heat for about 2 minutes on each side.

Turn down the heat and add the sake, umeboshi, sugar and ginger. Put the lid on, turn the heat to low and cook for 10 minutes. Remove the chicken and keep warm, and, if necessary, turn the heat up to reduce the sauce for a further minute. The umeboshi should have broken down now so you can remove the pits – the result should be a chunky, glossy, full-flavoured sauce that you can serve over the top of the chicken. Serve on a big bowl of warm, fluffy rice.

Note: *Umeboshi last forever so are a useful thing to have in the pantry. Once you've opened them, keep them in the fridge where they will continue everlasting. Eat them with rice, with pickles, or just save them for whenever you cook this wonderful dish, which will hopefully become a regular.*

あさりの酒蒸し

SAKE-STEAMED CLAMS

ASARI NO SAKAMUSHI

One of the quickest ways I can think of to get a delicious meal on the table is to steam clams – in this case they are steamed open with sake and warming fresh ginger. This is a popular appetiser that you might find on an izakaya menu, to be washed down with a glass of sake.

This is delicious on its own as a starter, or serve with steamed rice and some side dishes to make it into a meal.

SERVES 4 as a starter

700 g (1 lb 9 oz) clams
thumb-sized knob of ginger
2 spring onions (scallions)
2 teaspoons vegetable oil
60 ml (¼ cup) sake

Rinse and purge the clams of sand – to do this, place them in a large baking dish (so they're not too crowded) of fresh water with enough sea salt added to mimic seawater. Leave them to purge for 30 minutes.

In the meantime, cut the ginger into thin slices and then into matchsticks. Thinly slice the spring onions, keeping the green and white parts separate.

Warm a pan wide and deep enough to accommodate the clams over medium heat. Add the oil, ginger and white part of the onions and fry gently until the onion has wilted.

Add the drained clams, turn up the heat to high and pour in the sake, giving the pan a shake to distribute the clams. Put a lid on and leave to steam for 2–3 minutes, giving a shake every now and then to move the clams around. If they are piled on top of each other, they can have trouble opening.

Remove the lid to check on the clams – they may need another minute or two until they have all (or mostly all) opened. Pour onto a shallow serving dish with the juices and sprinkle with the spring onion tops.

医食同源「食べ物は薬」

Ishoku dogen: 'Food is medicine'

In Japan food is not just for sustenance: it is also something to help you feel better when you're under the weather, to help you cope with the heat, or even to cure colds and hangovers. In fact, there is a Japanese idiom imported from traditional Chinese medicine, *ishoku dogen* (医食同源), which translates to 'food and medicine, same origin', or 'food is medicine'.

From a cup of matcha tea to grilled eel on rice, to a warming kuzu yu or simple vinegar-dressed pickles and umeboshi (pickled plums), countless Japanese dishes are considered natural healing foods.

The fascinating account of Florentine merchant Francesco Carletti, who visited in 1597–98, makes it clear that the ishoku dogen philosophy was already practised in Japan in the 16th century. He was shocked to find the Japanese feeding their sick nutrient-rich foods rather than letting blood: 'What greater strangeness could there be than their way of caring for the sick, whom they feed on fresh and salted fish, as well as on telline [wedge clams] and other marine shellfish, and on various raw, sour, unripe fruits [umeboshi], and without ever letting blood, thus in everything doing the opposite of what we do?'

Traditional Chinese medicine came to Japan in the fifth century and was often practised by Buddhist monks. Extensive knowledge was passed between the two countries for about 1000 years until, gradually, a specific Japanese variation of Chinese medicine developed, called kampo. Part of this traditional medicine was the concept of food as medicine, or food therapy.

In 1713 the Japanese philosopher, physician and botanist Ekken Kaibara wrote one of his most well-known works, *Yojokun* (養生訓, *Instructions for Keeping Healthy*). It was a study of eating and drinking through his philosophical lens, greatly influenced by Confucianism and Buddhism. He was 83 years old when he wrote it, living proof of his healthy way of life. It includes advice such as: 'Sake is the nectar of heaven. It is extremely beneficial because just a little will cheer you up, calm hot-headedness, improve the appetite, and cause sorrow to be replaced by pleasure.'

Ekken was a champion of sencha for good health and recommended taking tea with rice in a dish called chameshi. Meaning 'tea rice', it is related to ochazuke (page 246): 'Pour sencha on top of rice, with red beans, black-eyed peas, broad beans, green peas, citrus peel, chestnuts, wild yam seeds and so on, heat and serve. It is good for the appetite and gives an open-chested happiness.' ●

豚の生姜焼き

GINGER PORK

SHOGAYAKI

This is a juicy, flavourful and extremely quick dish. The sake is the secret ingredient here – tenderising the pork and taking away any strong smells – while the ginger is the star.

This dish is said to help rejuvenate you when you're suffering fatigue, because the combination of pork and ginger creates a thiamine-rich meal. It's also ideal when you don't have much energy to cook, because it comes together in minutes. This is perfect on a bowl of freshly steamed rice to soak up the juices, perhaps with finely sliced raw cabbage or pickles, but you could add miso soup or another side dish to fill it out.

VARIATION: For a vegan version, use thin slices of eggplant (aubergine) or a meaty mushroom such as king brown.

SERVES 3–4

50 g (1¾ oz) ginger
2 tablespoons sake
300 g (10½ oz) pork loin, very thinly sliced
1 tablespoon soy sauce
1 tablespoon mirin
1 tablespoon sesame oil (or vegetable oil)
steamed rice (page 36), to serve

Peel and grate the ginger on a Japanese grater. You should find quite a bit of juice comes out – mix it with 1 tablespoon of the sake to marinate the pork while you get everything ready.

Mix the rest of the sake with the soy sauce, mirin and grated ginger in a bowl.

Heat the oil in a pan over high heat and cook the pork in batches for 1–2 minutes, flipping to cook both sides – this will be very quick as the slices are so thin. Add the sauce and bring to a rapid simmer for 1 minute, turning the pork to coat in the sauce. Remove the meat to a serving plate.

If you like, continue cooking the sauce in the pan for a minute to reduce it slightly. Pour over the pork and serve immediately on warm rice. The gingery sauce will flavour the rice so beautifully that, even after the pork is finished, it is still delicious on its own.

カステラ

CASTELLA CAKE

KASUTERA

Kasutera or castella cake is a uniquely Japanese sponge cake with a long history. It was originally brought to Japan by Portuguese merchants and missionaries in the middle of the 16th century. They were based in the port of Nagasaki and you can find bakeries there that have been carrying on the kasutera tradition for centuries – such as Fukusaya, founded in 1624, and Shooken, in 1681.

The name was borrowed from the Portuguese 'Pão de Castela', or 'bread from Castile' (in Spain). During the same period the Portuguese introduced other western dishes, ingredients and cooking techniques, such as tempura, nanbanzuke and konpeito (sugar confetti). Like these, kasutera has, over the centuries, become so ingrained in the country's cuisine that it is now considered a Japanese speciality, rather than 'yoshoku' (western-influenced Japanese cooking).

Today you can find it in many different variations, flavoured with chocolate, matcha, strawberry, peach or sakura (and tinted pink for spring). You will find a heartier egg-yolk version called gosan-yaki, which was beloved during the Edo period; more recently a wobbly, custardy Taiwanese version has become very popular. You can use kasutera to make fruit sandwiches – a popular, sweet version of the Japanese 'sando' – and you can use the batter to make the perfect dorayaki pancakes filled with anko (page 256).

One of the main characteristics of kasutera is its texture: it is moist yet has a good crumb, thanks to the use of a strong flour. Cake flour is lovely but makes it just a bit too soft, too similar to sponge cake. Another characteristic is, of course, its shape – perfectly rectangular. These cakes are usually baked in large square wooden boxes or trays – so the tops and bottoms are browned but not the sides – and then cut into individual long cakes. This is how they are still often sold: in beautiful wooden boxes, perfectly wrapped as a very special gift.

The original Nagasaki-style cakes have a crunch of zarame sugar (coarse white sugar), which is sprinkled over the base of the pan before putting the batter in – you can get a similar result with some raw (demerara) sugar. Another typical ingredient is mizuame, a starch or rice syrup, which keeps the cake moist and soft but can be difficult to find outside Japan.

For this homemade version, I find adding honey and mirin helps recreate the classic flavour and texture of what is otherwise just a simple egg, sugar and flour sponge.

MAKES 1 cake

raw (demerara) sugar, to sprinkle
6 eggs, at room temperature
100 g (3½ oz) sugar
200 g (1⅔ cups) bread flour
2 tablespoons honey (I like a strong, dark chestnut honey)
60 ml (¼ cup) mirin or sake

Heat the oven to 160°C (320°F) and line a loaf tin with baking paper. Sprinkle a little sugar over the base of the tin.

Beat the sugar and eggs until extremely pale and fluffy – this can take about 10 minutes with electric beaters, less with a stand mixer – just keep going until you see it change in colour, texture and volume. The batter should fall in ribbons.

Sift in the flour, and add the honey (if it's a bit stiff, warm it first) and mirin or sake. Stir well to combine any pockets of flour that might be hiding.

Pour into the tin and run a bamboo skewer up and down through the batter to burst any air bubbles. Give the tin a good tap on the counter to remove any bigger air bubbles.

Bake for 35–40 minutes or until deep golden brown and springy to the touch. Turn out onto a board and let it cool completely before cutting. When ready to serve, remove the paper and use a sharp bread knife to trim off the sides, leaving just the top and bottom browned crusts for a perfect kasutera look. Serve in thick slices.

酒粕チーズケーキ

RICOTTA & SAKE LEES CHEESECAKE

I first heard about sake lees cheesecake while visiting Masumi sake brewery in Nagano, and I couldn't wait to get home to try it myself! Sake lees gives this a distinct aroma and umami flavour that is difficult to describe, but could be compared to yoghurt.

I've resisted adding vanilla, lemon or other flavours to this that might compete or contrast with the sake lees. I wanted it to be the star, and for this to be the simplest kind of baked cheesecake possible: no fiddly crust, just throw everything into one bowl, mix and bake. It's perfect just with some fresh berries or other fruit.

If you'd like to give this a go but can't get sake lees, replace it with an extra 100 g (3½ oz) ricotta and 60 ml (¼ cup) aromatic premium drinking sake.

MAKES 1 cake

100 g (3½ oz) sake lees
150 g (5½ oz) fresh ricotta
250 g (9 oz) cream cheese
150 g (5½ oz) sugar
2 eggs, beaten
30 g (1 oz) rice flour (or potato starch), sifted

Heat the oven to 165°C (330°F). Butter and line a 20 cm (8 in) cake tin with baking paper.

If the sake lees is very compact and stiff, loosen it first, either by breaking it up with a fork or your hands or even whisking it. Do this in a large bowl, so you can then just add the rest of the ingredients. Whisk everything together until well combined and creamy. You might notice the little lumps of rice from the sake lees but otherwise it should be smooth.

Pour the batter into the tin and bake for 45–50 minutes or until golden brown with just the slightest wobble. Cool completely before serving.

甘酒

AMAZAKE

Amazake literally means 'sweet sake' and is a warming winter drink made of fermented rice that has a long history in Japan. Legend has it created by an eighth-century monk called Gyoki to cure the sick. For centuries it was considered a pick-me-up; even samurai warriors consumed amazake for strength before going into battle.

When you are huddled in a tea house, sipping on a cup of amazake to keep warm, it's easy to understand why the ancient people believed in the curative powers of this warm, nutritious drink. It's still served at festivals or temples, especially for the New Year, but you can also drink it iced in summer (like iced tea) or in smoothies.

There are two main ways to make amazake. The longer way is from scratch, beginning with rice (glutinous rice will give the creamiest results) and koji and leaving the mixture in a warm environment to ferment into a sweet drink. If you've ever made yoghurt at home, it's a similar process. The 'instant' way to make amazake is with sake lees – simply stir it into boiling water and add a touch of sugar or honey to your liking.

Either way, this is a comforting drink that also happens to be good for your digestion, thanks to the enzymes produced in the fermentation process. Note that sake lees is slightly alcoholic, so if you prefer no alcohol, do make sure to cook it longer.

SERVES 1

1 heaped tablespoon sake lees
150 ml (5 fl oz) water
1 teaspoon sugar
ground cinnamon or lemon zest (optional)

If the sake lees is quite firm, you might need to break it up or let it soak for a while first.

Put the sake lees, water and sugar in a small saucepan and bring to a simmer; give it a stir to ensure there are no large lumps other than soft little pieces of rice. If you're cooking the alcohol out of this, let it boil for 1 minute.

If you're adding cinnamon or lemon, add those and then remove from the heat. Your amazake is ready to drink.

酒サワー

SAKE SOUR COCKTAIL

Sake makes lovely cocktails. It has a relatively low alcohol content and delicate flavour, so it pairs well with other delicate flavours that don't overpower it. This is a deliciously light and refreshing citrus cocktail that my husband, Marco, came up with (before he was a sommelier, he was a cocktail barman at the Four Seasons Hotel in Florence). It would be perfect as a pre-dinner drink.

The sour is one of the world's most classic cocktails and is usually made with lemon or lime juice, a base liquor such as gin, whisky or rum, and egg white. The egg white creates an attractive layer of foam, but you can easily leave it out.

We have our own homemade umeshu, which I adore. Umeshu is often described as sweet 'plum wine' but is really an infusion of unripe ume – Japanese plums – with shochu and sugar. As I can't find ume here, I make it with little local Italian plums (while they're still green) and vodka, and leave it to infuse for three months. Then I dilute it a little to get it back to a similar alcohol level to shochu (around 25 per cent). In this cocktail it contributes to the sweetness and adds another layer of delicate flavour. If you cannot get umeshu, you could use amaretto or simply replace it with more sake.

The measures below are for classic cocktail jiggers, which are precisely for this purpose. If you don't have one, you can get creative – medicine cups have these small measures on them, too, or just take into account that 1 tablespoon is 15–20 ml and 1 teaspoon is about 5 ml.

SERVES 1

15 ml (½ fl oz) simple syrup (below)
40 ml (1¼ fl oz) sake
20 ml (¾ fl oz) umeshu
10 ml (¼ fl oz) yuzu juice
20 ml (¾ fl oz) lemon juice
15 ml (½ fl oz) egg white (optional)
ice

SIMPLE SYRUP
1 tablespoon sugar
1 tablespoon water

For the simple syrup, combine the sugar and water and heat until the sugar dissolves, then leave to cool. There will be a little more than you need for this recipe.

Put all the ingredients into a cocktail shaker, filling it up with ice, and shake vigorously for about 10 seconds. Strain into a glass and serve immediately.

お屠蘇

SPICED SAKE FOR NEW YEAR

OTOSO

This special infusion is served before you begin your osechi meal on New Year's Day, starting from the youngest drinker to the eldest, and is said to ward off any illness for the coming year. As my friend and long-time Tokyo resident Jessica Thompson writes for *Appetite Press*: 'At the core of otoso is a cocktail of herbs and spices (known as *tosoan*), which are curated to dispel the ill-health of the past and wish for good health in the year to come. The kanji (屠蘇) represents "slaughtering evil" and "reviving the soul", a corpse reviver of sorts – just what many of us need at the time of year.'

The tradition was adopted from China in the ninth century, during the reign of Emperor Saga. As John Gauntner recounts, on 19 December eight medicinal herbs would be placed in a bag and hung from the branch of a peach tree over water. At 4am on New Year's Day, the herbs were steeped in sake for a few hours before being consumed.

In the traditional ritual, the otoso is poured from a special teapot-like vessel into stacked red-lacquered sake cups, like the ones used for the wedding sake ceremony. The youngest drinker begins, in order to the eldest, so that 'the older members of the family can share in the joy of youth imparted as the cups are passed', explains Gauntner. The tradition is that if the entire family drinks otoso, their whole village will remain free from illness for the year.

By the Edo period (1603–1868), families began making their own otoso bags (otosoan) rather than getting them from pharmacies, as had been the practice. Today you can get them in beautiful packages from the pharmacy, and even buy otoso bags from konbini (convenience stores). Of course, you can custom-design your own herb selection.

Some of the herbs include: cinnamon (good for the heart and digestion); rhubarb root (to aid digestion); sansho pepper (antibacterial); china root (*Smilax china*, used to combat inflammation); goji berries and dried mandarin or yuzu peel (to boost the immune system); cloves (good for the liver); ginger (good for circulation and fighting colds); bellflower root (for inflammation); kikyo (*Platycodi radix*, for respiratory illnesses); kuromoji (an aromatic plant in the bay family); star anise (good for digestion); and licorice root (to soothe the throat). Use as many as you like, just remember to use the whole version of the spice (cinnamon sticks, whole cloves) rather than a ground version.

The sweetness of mirin offsets the bitterness of the herbs and spices, so otoso is made traditionally with a ratio of one-to-one mirin to sake, but I prefer more sake to mirin. I recommend trying this if you can find a very nice drinking mirin.

SERVES 4–5

60 ml (¼ cup) hon-mirin
250 ml (1 cup) sake
1 cinnamon stick
pinch of whole cloves
1 slice ginger (dried or fresh)
pinch of sansho pepper
1 piece mandarin peel (dry or fresh), chopped
2–3 cm (1 in) licorice root
3 dried goji berries
1 bay leaf

Put everything in a teapot or jug and let it steep for 4 to 8 hours at room temperature – the longer it steeps, the stronger the herbs and spices will be. Strain and serve at room temperature.

米酢

RICE VINEGAR

米酢

RICE VINEGAR

'Vinegar is good for a tired body.'

MY OBAACHAN

Just as vinegar is linked to wine-making, so is rice vinegar linked to sake brewing. The character for vinegar, *su*, 酢, tells you this – the left radical means 'sake', and the right means 'to make'.

The history of Japanese rice vinegar began when brewing rice for alcohol was introduced to Japan in the fourth or fifth century – sake and vinegar were made alongside one another. But it took another 1000 years for rice vinegar to become a common seasoning. Perhaps because of this, it wasn't until the later part of the Edo period (1603–1868) that vinegar dishes such as nigiri sushi started to spread across the country. For many centuries rice vinegar was treated as a luxury, reserved only for the aristocracy.

During the Second World War, and in its aftermath, Japan suffered devastating shortages of, in particular, rice, the country's staple, which meant that sake, mirin and rice vinegar were also affected. To save what little rice there was for eating, the production of mirin and vinegar using rice was banned. Similarly to what happened to mirin, a replacement synthetic rice vinegar was developed from petroleum and limestone. But, while artificial mirin became more popular than the real deal, rice vinegar eventually returned to being made with rice and, thankfully, the synthetic version is rare today.

There is rice vinegar and *rice vinegar*, though. Mass-produced rice vinegar can be made in a matter of hours, with a bare minimum of 40 g (1½ oz) rice per litre of vinegar. Other grains are allowed in this category too, according to Japanese Agricultural Standards (JAS), but it is not generally possible to make rice vinegar with this amount of rice, so manufacturers often add ethanol. 'Pure rice vinegar' requires a minimum of 120 g (4½ oz) rice per litre of vinegar; but, the more rice used, the better quality and more flavoured the vinegar.

For pure rice vinegar, a double fermentation process takes place. Steamed rice inoculated with koji is the start of the rice vinegar process, just as for sake. The koji breaks down the starch into sugar, which is then converted to alcohol. This is sake. But what turns this sake into vinegar is the next step, the second fermentation, when acetic acid bacteria is added in the form of a 'mother' of pure rice vinegar; this converts the alcohol into rice vinegar. It is matured for a further month or so, for flavour, and then filtered and bottled.

I visited Japan's oldest vinegar distillery, Onomichizousu, founded in 1582, to understand more about the process. It is in the charming town of Onomichi, not far from Hiroshima in southern Japan. There were once many vinegar-makers in this lively merchant town, which also has a rich vinegar-based cuisine. The climate here is mild and, thanks to the Seto Inland Sea, it doesn't get too cold, which makes it the perfect environment for rice vinegar.

This small but thriving port town was strategically located on the Edo period's kitamae-bune shipping route from Osaka, through the Inland Sea, to Hokkaido, meaning the vinegar producers not only had access to high-quality rice from the north, but also that their vinegar could be shipped easily around the country. Some of the old ceramic crocks used for shipping vinegar are still in the Onomichizousu distillery.

Zenyou Tanakamaru, the executive officer of Onomichizousu, generously took me around the distillery. They use what is called a horizontal continuous fermentation method, which they patented in the 1950s. This requires a lot of time and labour and constant daily supervision. We climb up wooden stairs through the oldest surviving part of the factory, held up by 400-year-old beams. One of the reasons they can call themselves the oldest vinegar factory in the country is sheer luck: they have been spared earthquakes and atomic bombs.

We arrive at the top room, which is filled with long, thin tanks shimmering with liquid that is covered by a matte web-like skin. It is the precious sakusan-kin, acetic bacteria. 'This is the most important room in the factory,' Mr Tanakamaru explains, beaming proudly. 'The acetic acid bacteria that still live here today have seen over 440 years of history.' This is the key ingredient to making vinegar and they look after it 365 days of the year to ensure it stays healthy.

The vinegar made here uses a slightly different method from the sake-to-vinegar process. Here they use sake lees – the mash that's left over after filtering sake – from a local Hiroshima brewery. This is aged for three years until it turns a miso-like colour; then it's dissolved in their mineral-rich well water and filtered. This liquid goes into the horizontal fermentation tanks in contact with the acetic acid bacteria, which flows down very slowly at a slight angle. The bacteria convert the alcohol from the sake lees into vinegar, which ferments naturally at its own pace. It takes six months to make vinegar this way and then it is aged for a further six months to enhance its flavour and fragrance.

但馬の
赤酢
醸造酢
AKAZU
三年熟成
福山甕酢
KUROZU
有機
純米酢
KOMEZU
ORANGE VINEGAR

WHAT TO LOOK FOR

Japanese rice vinegar has a mild acidity, less than five per cent acetic acid. Like soy sauce, it's quite a different product from rice vinegars offered in other Asian nations – they are not interchangeable. This is indispensable in a Japanese kitchen for pickling, making sushi and flavouring sauces and dressings. Its sweetness and mildness makes it difficult to find an appropriate substitute – other vinegars are just too strong.

Rice vinegar has long had the important role of preserving food – in particular, rice and fish – while vegetables are seasoned with it more for eating right away. It also adds umami, aroma and an uplifting flavour to dishes, balancing out sweetness or saltiness, both of which are well used in Japanese cooking.

Rice vinegar is also highly appreciated for its nutritional value – it is known to help regulate blood sugars, improve circulation and work as an appetite stimulant. My obaachan always told me to eat something containing vinegar to give me energy when I'm feeling tired and fatigued, especially in summer.

TYPES OF VINEGAR

Kokumotsusu (穀物酢) is a grain vinegar, which can be made with rice or barley and sake lees and is one of the most common types available.

Komezu (米酢) is a mild, sweet rice vinegar. It is clear (sometimes slightly yellow) so will not affect the colour of a dish (such as rice for sushi rice).

You might also come across sushi vinegar, **sushizu** (すし酢), which is rice vinegar seasoned with salt, sugar and sometimes dashi. (It is also easy to make at home, see page 194.)

There is also a dark brown rice vinegar, made from unpolished rice, which is known as black vinegar or **kurozu** (黒酢). This has an interestingly robust flavour, and many times the quantity of amino acids of regular vinegar (amino acids = umami), so it's also a particularly nutritious vinegar. The production method is interesting too – it is left to age in pots by the sea, out in the open air in Kagoshima prefecture on Kyushu Island.

Red vinegar, or **akazu** (赤酢), is an Edo period-style vinegar, made from aged sake lees that has become brown over time and developed major umami flavours. After aging for a few years, it is mixed with water, acetic bacteria and then fermented for a few more months and left to mature again. It is then filtered and bottled. This has very mild acidity and a red colour.

Fruit vinegars are also popular in Japan, including those made with figs, apples, persimmons and bitter oranges. At Onomichizousu they make vinegar with surplus fruit and peels that would otherwise be thrown away. They also work very closely with local farmers, such as Onomichi Kakien, a wonderful persimmon farm in the nearby mountains.

HOW TO STORE VINEGAR

Keeping vinegar couldn't be easier: just ensure it remains in a cool, dark place. You can keep bottles of vinegar for years; it doesn't ever go bad.

甘酢漬け

SWEET PICKLES

AMAZUZUKE

This type of pickling, meaning 'sweet vinegar', is one of the most basic types of Japanese pickle. Salt draws out excess liquid from the vegetables, which are pickled in a liquid of sugar and rice vinegar of varying proportions, according to taste. These are ideal for eating right away, making this more like a salad dressing than a western pickle.

A great example, which most people have probably tasted in a sushi shop, is gari, or pickled ginger. Another one is namasu, a special dish of julienned carrots and daikon made for New Year celebrations. In fact, the earliest documentation of a pickle recipe is in the *Manyoshu* anthology of poetry from the eighth century, describing namasu.

The proportions for amazuzuke can be one-to-one (sugar to vinegar), or one-to-two. However, I often find even this too sweet, particularly with certain vegetables that are already sweet, such as carrots, so I tend to use less sugar. I like raw sugar best for pickles, but use white sugar if that's what you have.

The key is to taste the pickling liquid: it should be a balance of sweet and very delicately acidic. Rice vinegar is key here for that very reason; it's naturally sweet and mellow and not as sharp as western vinegars.

VARIATION: You can use any vegetables here. Root vegetables such as daikon, turnips and carrots are particularly good, but also try napa cabbage, ginger, or a mix.

FILLS 1 x 250 ml (1 cup) jar

200 g (7 oz) radishes or cucumbers
pinch of salt
2 tablespoons rice vinegar
2–3 teaspoons raw (demerara) or white sugar

Top and tail the radishes and finely slice. Place in a bowl with a good three-fingered pinch of salt and mix really well. Leave for 5–10 minutes.

Stir together the vinegar and sugar in a small bowl to dissolve the sugar. If you're in a hurry, you can heat this to help it along. Taste, adding more sugar if you like.

The vegetables should have released some liquid: drain them, rinse in fresh water and drain again. Pat dry on a clean tea towel (not a white one, the radishes bleed pink!) and put in a jar, container or resealable bag with the sweet vinegar. The liquid doesn't need to fill the jar or even cover all the vegetables: it's more like a dressing

Eat right away or keep in the fridge for several days. Taste and add a bit more salt, if you like. If you do keep in the jar, give it a turn every now and then – the resealable plastic bag is also useful for this.

中川屋
1pc
500円
2本
300円
千枚漬
一夜漬
一夜漬
要冷蔵
要冷蔵
宮川食品のあさづけ
国産

らっきょう

PICKLED JAPANESE SCALLION

RAKKYO

Another kind of amazuzuke, this is the classic accompaniment to Japanese curry (page 82). Rakkyo has a rather strong flavour and my relatives in Japan used to be surprised that I loved these as a child; I guess it was the beginning of my love for all the allium family. In fact, rakkyo is *Allium chinense*, which goes by many names: Chinese garlic, Chinese onion, glittering chive and Japanese scallion, to name a few. It has a prominent bulb with thin stalks that look like spring onions.

As you can imagine, rakkyo is related to garlic, spring onions, leeks – all those delicious alliums. So, if you cannot find *Allium chinense*, use spring onions or Italian cipollotti, which is what I can find where I live.

In Japan rakkyo is much appreciated for its health benefits, especially its positive effects on the digestive system – perhaps that is why it is always served with curry.

FILLS 1 x 250 ml (1 cup) jar

- **200 g (7 oz) Japanese scallion bulbs, or spring onions (scallions)**
- **125 ml (½ cup) rice vinegar**
- **3 tablespoons raw (demerara) or white sugar**
- **2 teaspoons salt**
- **1 dried or fresh chilli pepper, thinly sliced (optional)**

Clean the onion bulbs, trimming off the roots and, if necessary, peeling off the first layer. By 'bulbs' you're looking at the first 3–4 cm (1½ in). Blanch them in a pan of boiling water for 1 minute, then drain.

Heat the vinegar, sugar and salt in a small pan to dissolve the sugar, then allow to cool. Taste to see if the liquid is balanced: you could add more sugar if you feel it is too acidic.

Put the rakkyo in a jar with the chilli, if using, and cover with the pickling liquid. Leave to pickle for 24 hours and then enjoy. These last quite well for the week in the fridge; unless they are all eaten first, that is.

大根のビール漬け

HAMA-SAN'S DAIKON BEER PICKLES

DAIKON NO BIIRUZUKE

I was served these sweet pickles while visiting the steep mountain home of Hama-san, a sprightly, 80-year-old tea farmer in the tiny township of Tenryu, Nagano. My mother and I joined her to make yubeshi (page 90) with the new-season yuzu. After lunch we visited the tea terraces next to her house – the yuzu trees standing over them are so tall that neither she nor the forest monkeys can get to the fruit at the top.

It was a very memorable lunch and I spied about 30 huge daikon in the garden, waiting to get pickled. Hama-san's pickles are extremely good and she generously gave me the recipe. This makes enough to fill a jam jar, but you can easily double or even, as Hama-san does, multiply the amounts by ten!

FILLS 1 x 250 ml (1 cup) jar

200 g (7 oz) daikon
¼ teaspoon salt
50 g (¼ cup) sugar
1½ tablespoons beer
60 ml (¼ cup) rice vinegar

Cut the daikon into 1–2 mm (⅛ in) slices and, if particularly large, you can also cut into quarters. Put in a bowl and toss with a pinch of salt. Leave for about 10 minutes – the salt will draw out some moisture. Rinse the daikon in fresh water, pat dry and place in a jar.

Warm the salt, sugar, beer and vinegar in a small saucepan and simmer until the sugar dissolves (this also removes the alcohol from the beer). Cool before pouring over the top of the daikon. Keep in the fridge. Hama-san says to let it marinate for 4 days before serving.

スイカの皮の漬物

PICKLED WATERMELON RIND

SUIKA NO KAWA NO TSUKEMONO

We eat a lot of watermelon in this house, all summer long. This is a delicious 'mottainai' (no waste) recipe and a fantastic way to not throw away so much of the watermelon rind.

The important thing here is to cut away as much of the pink watermelon as you can (it is full of water and can dilute the pickling liquid), and also the tough green rind. You are pickling mainly the white part, which, in the end, tastes like its cousin, the cucumber. (You could use cucumbers for this recipe too.)

FILLS 1 x 250 ml (1 cup) jar

300 g (10½ oz) watermelon rind

2 teaspoons soy sauce

2 teaspoons rice vinegar

2 teaspoons sesame oil

pinch of sugar

1 teaspoon sesame seeds

Trim the watermelon rind of any pink or green parts, leaving just the white. Chop into bite-sized pieces. Toss together with the rest of the ingredients.

This is at its best right away or kept in a jar in the fridge and eaten within 2 days – the longer it pickles, the more the watermelon will water down the pickling liquid.

和風 サラダ

WAFU SALAD

WAFU SARADA

This is a typical Japanese-style dressing with a western-style garden salad. You'll find a salad similar to this served all over Japan in all kinds of meals, from breakfast to bento. This is a sweet vinegar-based dressing with some oomph from the soy sauce and is also good as a seasoning with simply boiled or steamed vegetables or tofu.

Some might add grated onion to this – you'll find that version bottled as a quick salad topping – and I like it with a kick of grated fresh ginger.

VARIATION: You can, of course, adjust the salad ingredients: try different varieties of lettuce; thinly sliced raw red onion; shiso; shredded carrot; raw daikon cut into matchsticks; or finely chopped spring onions (scallions).

SERVES 4

handful of baby spinach
handful of shredded cabbage
handful of mung beans
8 cherry tomatoes, halved
⅓ long cucumber, thinly sliced
4 radishes, sliced

DRESSING
2 teaspoons soy sauce
2 teaspoons rice vinegar
1 teaspoon olive oil
½ teaspoon sugar
2 cm (¾ in) piece of ginger, grated (optional)

Combine the dressing ingredients, taste and adjust any of the seasonings, if you like. Arrange the salad ingredients in a bowl and pour over the dressing. Serve immediately.

夏野菜の土佐酢づけ

SUMMER VEGETABLE TOSAZUZUKE

NATSU YASAI NO TOSAZUZUKE

This is a great summer dish – you can make a big batch, put it in the fridge and enjoy over a few days without having to cook.

Tosazu is basically a dashi vinegar – a delicious smoky condiment of rice vinegar, soy sauce, mirin and katsuobushi. Its name means 'Tosa-style vinegar' – Tosa, known for its smoky katsuobushi, was the ancient name of Kochi prefecture on the island of Shikoku. It is also famous for tosashoyu, which, you might be able to guess, is soy sauce with katsuobushi in it.

Tosazu is a sanbaizu dressing, a Japanese sunomono dressing made with a three-two-one ratio of rice vinegar, sugar and soy sauce, similar to that in sanbaizu bonito (page 198).

VARIATIONS: For a vegetarian version, simply leave out the katsuobushi flakes. If you can get them, shio kombu (dried salted kombu strips) could be a great addition instead. You can use any favourite summer vegetables here – okra and red or green bell peppers are also great.

SERVES 3–4

1 long Japanese eggplant (aubergine), sliced
2–3 shishito peppers or 1 green pepper (capsicum)
1 long cucumber, sliced
6 cherry tomatoes, halved
spring onions (scallions), thinly sliced, to garnish

SAUCE

3 tablespoons rice vinegar
2 tablespoons mirin or sugar
1 tablespoon soy sauce
good pinch of katsuobushi flakes

Heat a dry cast-iron pan, or even a barbecue, and gently brown the eggplant and peppers on both sides. Leave to cool, then place in a shallow dish with the cucumber and tomatoes.

Heat the vinegar, mirin and soy sauce in a small pan until the sauce is beginning to simmer and the sugar, if using, has dissolved. Add the katsuobushi and immediately turn off the heat and let it steep like a tea.

After 5 minutes, strain to remove the katsuobushi and pour over the vegetables. Leave in the fridge for a couple of hours to marinate (it will keep in there for several days) and enjoy chilled, garnished with the spring onions.

マグロのぬた

TUNA IN MISO-VINEGAR

MAGURO NO NUTA

Nuta is a miso-vinegar dressing that, although it might be a bit old-fashioned, I think is one of the most delicious combinations ever. My grandmother often made this with squid. Raw tuna makes it an especially quick preparation. This is typically eaten as a little appetiser with sake.

Sometimes I crave nuta and – not having any seafood to put in it – I've made it with the spring onions only. It's still delicious, because it's all really just a vehicle to enjoying the miso-vinegar sauce!

If you like a bit of heat, a pea-sized addition of wasabi is highly recommended. Wasabi miso-vinegar (wasabi miso-su, 山葵味噌酢) is its own thing, a dressing that you can even find in the 1643 cookbook *Ryori Monogatari*. The brief instructions say: 'Grate wasabi. Add miso. Knead it well, then dilute with vinegar.' Hot Japanese mustard (similar to hot English mustard) is a very good addition to this if you don't have wasabi, or even some freshly grated ginger for a more subtle heat.

VARIATIONS: Use boiled squid, peeled cooked prawns, or even clams instead of tuna; try tinned tuna or mackerel as well. For a vegan version, simply leave out the tuna – I love that spring onions get their moment to be the star of the show!

SERVES 2–4 as a starter

- **1 bunch of spring onions (scallions)**
- **150 g (5½ oz) sashimi grade tuna, cut into 1 cm (½ in) cubes**
- **2 tablespoons white miso**
- **1 tablespoon rice vinegar**
- **1 tablespoon sugar**
- **¼ teaspoon wasabi (optional)**
- **1 teaspoon toasted sesame seeds**

Trim the spring onions of their roots and very tops. Cut the stalks into 3 cm (about 1 in) sections. Bring a small saucepan of water to the boil and blanch the spring onions for 1 minute, or until wilted. Drain, rinse under cold water, drain again and pat dry.

Combine the spring onions with the tuna, miso, vinegar, sugar and wasabi (if using) and stir to coat well. Sprinkle with sesame seeds and serve immediately, before the vinegar pickles the tuna.

南蛮かぼちゃ

NANBAN PUMPKIN

NANBAN KABOCHA

Nanban means 'southern barbarian' and was a term used to describe the foreigners who arrived in southern Japan in the 16th century. They were Portuguese merchants and missionaries, who introduced dishes such as tempura, castella (page 158) and even bread.

This dish is nothing more than an escabeche – a Spanish and Portuguese preparation that made its way around the world wherever they went. It is usually made with fish (I love it with mackerel or salmon) that is first dusted in flour, fried and then marinated in vinegar to make it long lasting. It's also delicious with seasonal vegetables, such as eggplant (aubergine) in the summer, instead of the autumn or winter pumpkin.

Japanese pumpkin (known as kabocha) or the Italian mantovana variety, which is very sweet and floury with edible skin, are both perfect for this; otherwise, use butternut, which you will need to peel.

SERVES 4

300 g (10½ oz) pumpkin (peeled, if necessary)
2 tablespoons potato starch
2 tablespoons olive oil
good pinch of salt
½ carrot, peeled and cut into matchsticks
½ onion, thinly sliced
1 hot chilli, thinly sliced
½ lemon, thinly sliced

MARINADE

80 ml (⅓ cup) rice wine vinegar
2 tablespoons soy sauce
2 tablespoons mirin
1 tablespoon sake
3 tablespoons water or dashi (pages 108–9)

Preheat the oven to 180°C (350°F). Cut the pumpkin into 1 cm (½ in) slices and then into pieces that can be easily picked up with chopsticks. Dust lightly in potato starch.

Place the pumpkin on a baking tray, drizzle with olive oil and season with salt. Bake for about 15 minutes until tender.

To make the marinade, heat all the ingredients in a saucepan and simmer for 2–3 minutes.

When the pumpkin is cooked, place in a deep ceramic or glass dish or similar. Scatter with the carrot, onion and chilli. Pour on the warm marinade and top with the lemon slices.

Leave for at least 30 minutes, but overnight if you can. You can eat this warm or cold and it keeps very well in the fridge for several days.

しめ鯖の箱ずし

PRESSED SUSHI WITH MARINATED MACKEREL

SHIMESABA NO HAKOZUSHI

Shimesaba is vinegar-marinated raw mackerel. The vinegar changes the appearance and texture of the fish, making it seem cooked – the word shime (しめ) comes from the verb to 'firm up'. This is one of my favourite kinds of sashimi. It is simple to make and is even delicious as is, with a bowl of rice and some pickles.

Hakozushi is a kind of pressed sushi, one of the oldest kinds of sushi, and with different regional variations. In Aichi prefecture it's presented with an array of different colourful foods on top. Other typical toppings are cooked chopped prawns, eel and salted salmon, or vegetables such as thinly sliced cucumber, wilted spinach or wild greens.

This type of sushi gets its name from the wooden box (hako) that it is pressed in to create its shape and make it easy to cut and transport. It was a very luxurious dish in early times because rice was very expensive. But it was something made at home and it was quite common to own hako, especially for this.

With the rise of sushi shops, hakozushi became less common and not everyone has a hako anymore. You really don't need any special materials to make this; you can do it in a bento box or any rectangular container you have. I use my 23 x 18 cm (9 x 7 in) tofu mould, which is perfect for this as you can lift the top sides off; but plastic wrap, baking paper or even haran leaves (*Aspidistra elatior*) will help you handle the sticky rice.

MAKES 12 pieces

SHIMESABA

100 g (3½ oz) mackerel fillets (see note)
pinch of salt
60 ml (¼ cup) rice vinegar

For the shimesaba, clean the defrosted mackerel fillets with paper towel and pat dry. Sprinkle on both sides with a generous pinch of salt and rub this in. Place in the fridge for 30 minutes, then rinse and pat dry. Place in a container, skin-side-up, and pour the vinegar over them.

Leave to marinate for at least 30 minutes and up to 2 hours. If they are very thick, they may need longer. You will see the fish turn opaque when it has been marinated long enough. Remove from the marinade, pat dry. Now remove any bones you see, and remove the thin transparent membrane on the skin – to do this, just peel it from the corner furthest from the tail and pull up. These are ready now – keep covered in the fridge until needed.

Continued ›

SUSHI RICE

60 ml (¼ cup) rice vinegar

1½ tablespoons sugar

1½ teaspoons salt

3 cups (555g) freshly steamed rice (page 36)

TOPPINGS

3–4 dried shiitake mushrooms

2 teaspoons soy sauce

2 teaspoons sugar

2 eggs

pinch of salt

vegetable oil, for greasing

For the sushi rice, make a sushizu (sushi dressing) by heating the vinegar, sugar and salt in a small pan until the sugar dissolves – don't boil it. If you're making this ahead, it will keep in the fridge for 3 weeks.

Put the warm, freshly cooked rice in a wide bowl or tray and dress with the sushizu, starting with about 1 tablespoon. Mix with a rice paddle (or spatula) in a cutting motion so you don't crush the rice grains. It helps to fan with one hand while you do this with the other so that the extra moisture evaporates. Only add another tablespoon of sushizu when the previous spoonful has been absorbed; keep mixing and fanning until it is done.

Sushi rice should be sticky, glistening and – taste some – well seasoned. Add a bit more sushizu if you feel you need, but make sure you don't end up with soggy rice. You can leave it covered with a damp tea towel or plastic wrap at room temperature. Sushi rice should never be put in the fridge – the grains will harden and be ruined.

For the toppings, soak the shiitake mushrooms in hot water for 20 minutes. Drain, keeping the soaking water. Remove the stems and finely slice the caps, then put in a small pan with the soy sauce and sugar. Add enough of the soaking water (filter, if necessary) to just cover. Simmer for about 10 minutes, until the liquid is almost completely gone.

Mix the eggs with a pinch of salt and scramble them in a lightly greased pan. You want very well-cooked, fluffy scrambled eggs, like little mimosa flowers.

To assemble the hakozushi, place some haran leaves, plastic wrap or baking paper on the bottom, letting it come up the sides. Start with a 2–3 cm (1 in) layer of sushi rice on the bottom. On top place 2 mackerel fillets on the diagonal, about 5 cm (2 in) apart. Now decorate the empty spaces of rice with shiitake mushroom and the eggs. Cover with paper/plastic wrap and the top of the wooden press, applying pressure. Leave a weight on top for 5–10 minutes.

If using a bento box or other container, after lining and layering, line the top of the sushi and find any flat, heavy object that fits to press the rice with – a heavy glass or tin of tomatoes, for example.

Lift up the sushi and place on a chopping board. Cut into small portions, using your sharpest knife and wiping with a wet tea towel in between for clean cuts.

Note: *Use extremely fresh whole mackerel for this – you will need 1 small mackerel. Fillet it (or have your fishmonger do it for you), then put the fillets in your freezer for at least 4 days, defrosting before you cook. The freezing ensures any potential parasites (anisakis) are eliminated – it's a very small chance you would come across them, but it is better to be safe than sorry.*

鶏のさっぱり煮

VINEGAR-BRAISED CHICKEN

TORI NO SAPPARINI

Sappari means 'refreshing' and that is exactly what the vinegar does to this braise – it gives it an incredible, sweet-and-sour flavour that is fresh and delicious. Black vinegar is particularly good here. This is one of those dishes that just gets better the next day – and the day after that.

Serve this with some rice and perhaps simple greens or a salad. The boiled eggs add some extra protein and make this a satisfying, filling meal, but you can leave them out if you are not a fan. To soft-boil eggs, boil them straight from the fridge (I always forget to bring to room temperature first). If you're using 55 g (2 oz) eggs, cook for 7 minutes for jammy eggs and 8 minutes if you like them slightly more set. They will continue cooking in the sauce a little here, so the shorter time should be fine.

VARIATION: Boiled daikon and firm tofu, eggplant (aubergine) slices or king brown mushrooms would be wonderful cooked this way, too, if you are looking for a vegetarian or vegan alternative to the chicken.

SERVES 3–4

12 chicken wings
vegetable oil, for greasing
1 garlic clove, sliced
3 cm (about 1 in) piece of ginger, sliced
125 ml (½ cup) rice vinegar
60 ml (¼ cup) sake
60 ml (¼ cup) water
2 teaspoons soy sauce
2 teaspoons raw (demerara) sugar
4 soft-boiled eggs, peeled
steamed rice (page 36), to serve

Cut the chicken wings and separate the drumettes and tips. Heat a casserole pot or frying pan and oil it lightly. Brown the wings over medium–high heat for about 10 minutes, until browned on all sides.

Turn the heat to low and add the garlic, ginger, vinegar, sake, water, soy sauce and sugar. Cover the pan and cook for 10 minutes, then turn the chicken and add the eggs.

Cook for another 5 minutes, then uncover the pan, turn the eggs so they colour evenly and cook uncovered to reduce the sauce for a few minutes before serving with freshly steamed rice. Leftovers will keep in the fridge for several days.

かつお三杯酢

SANBAIZU BONITO

KATSUO SANBAIZU

Sanbaizu is a Japanese sunomono dressing made with a three-two-one ratio of rice vinegar, sugar and soy sauce. The name comes from an old way of measuring the number of bowls: sanbai means three bowls. You can use sanbaizu as a dressing, a marinade, or for pickles: it's very versatile and such an easy ratio to remember. This is also delicious as a savoury topping for chilled kanten jelly noodles.

Like shimesaba (page 192), marinating in vinegar not only makes the fish last longer here, but also gives it an extra special umami flavour. I love this with bonito, which is called palamita in Italian and is abundant in the Mediterranean – it has a dark, firm flesh reminiscent of tuna.

VARIATIONS: You could use any firm fish – kingfish, tuna or salmon would work well. For a vegan version, use thick slices of eggplant (aubergine).

SERVES 4

400 g (14 oz) bonito fillets
3 tablespoons potato starch or plain (all-purpose) flour
1 tablespoon vegetable oil
1 hot chilli, finely sliced (optional)

SANBAIZU
3 tablespoons rice vinegar
2 tablespoons raw (demerara) sugar
1 tablespoon soy sauce

Run your fingers along the bonito fillets and remove any bones you can feel, then cut into 4 cm (1½ in) pieces. Dust in the starch.

Heat the oil in a frying pan over medium heat and fry the fish on both sides for 2–3 minutes on each side, or until perfectly cooked through. Place in a deep ceramic or glass dish.

Combine the sanbaizu ingredients in a small pan and heat until the sugar dissolves. Pour over the fish and sprinkle with chilli, if using.

Serve right away or leave to marinate for a few hours in the fridge or even overnight. You can eat this cold or warmed up – it will keep for several days, getting better with each day.

胡麻
SESAME

胡麻
SESAME

'What is Buddha?' 'Three pounds of sesame.'

ZEN BUDDHIST KOAN

This ninth century koan – a story or question from Zen Buddhist lore to meditate upon – is mentioned in *Instructions for the Cook* (*Tenzo Kyokun*, 典座教訓), written in 1237 by the Japanese monk Eihei Dogen. It is a famous Zen manual on the running of a monastery kitchen and the symbolism of cooking.

The reference to this particular koan is to show how everyday activities and working with everyday ingredients are no less important than a spiritual awakening, when they are done with a clear mind. Dogen offers instructions for taking care with every action, no matter how seemingly mundane: 'The tenzo [cook] should always be present at the sink when the rice is being soaked and the water measured. Watching with clear eyes, ensure that not a single grain is wasted. Washing it well, place it in the pots, make a fire, and boil it. An old teacher said: "Regard the cooking pot as your own head, the water your own life-blood."'

Sesame (goma, 胡麻) – usually as a representation of something ordinary, cheap and simple – appears in other Zen koans too, such as this one from the important *Blue Cliff Records* (written in 1125): A monk asked Zen master Ummon Bun'en, 'What is the teaching that transcends god and patriarchs?' Ummon said, 'A sesame bun'.

In fact, as humble as sesame might be considered, it has long been appreciated in Asian cultures for its health properties. Sesame seeds were said to hold the secret of longevity; in fact, their properties have been widely studied by scientists and are known to be anti-aging, antioxidant, anticancer, antidiabetic and anti-inflammatory, thanks to sesame lignan (the same substance that makes sesame oil so long lasting).

Because of its high nutrient content, sesame has always been an important ingredient in Zen Buddhist cooking (Japan's no-waste temple cuisine, page 226) as a protein supplement for this vegetable-based cuisine. Even the act of making sesame paste by hand, with a traditional suribachi (similar to a mortar and pestle), is considered a worthy Zen practice – goma dofu (sesame 'tofu' page 224) is the ultimate dish for this.

Sesame is prized in Japanese cooking for its aromatic oil and its seeds, which are added to many everyday dishes (the black seeds, in particular, are popular in sweets and baked goods) and ground into a dark, robust paste, not too different from tahini.

An annual grass, native to Sub-Saharan Africa, sesame seems to have been first cultivated by humans 3000 to 4000 years ago around the Nile River. This is still where most sesame comes from today, along with India, Myanmar, China and South America.

There are many wild types of sesame, but there is just one cultivated sesame plant, *Sesamum indicum*. Of this hardy and drought-resistant crop, there are approximately 3000 varieties. In temperate climates like Japan's, the seeds are sown in early summer and grow quickly with the hot weather. Pretty trumpet-shaped flowers begin to bloom 40 to 50 days after sowing and then, once these have fallen, pods full of seeds are produced. These are harvested before the pods get a chance to ripen fully and release the seeds. The long-stemmed bunches of sesame grasses are bundled and hung to dry, then threshed to collect the seeds.

The seeds are pressed to obtain an abundant and nutrient-rich oil, rich in essential fatty acids and protein. (Sesame oil has been used for lighting lamps even longer than for cooking.) Depending on the style of oil, the seeds might be roasted – similar to coffee beans – before pressing. Other than heightening the flavour and darkening the colour, roasting also increases the antioxidants.

Sesame likely arrived in Japan via China, where it was discovered thanks to the Chinese explorer and diplomat, Zhang Qian, who was sent west along the Silk Road to initiate trade in the second century BC. Along with pomegranates and walnuts, sesame was one of the important foods he brought back to China. It has also been considered that sesame perhaps found its way to Japan as early as the late Jomon period (14,000–300 BC) – I wonder if this could have been egoma wild sesame (opposite).

Either way, sesame as a food spread through China and Japan thanks to Buddhism. Because the religion prohibited the killing of animals, sesame was a nutritious and delicious replacement for meat. In Japan the earliest written documentation of sesame crops dates to the ninth century. According to William Shurtleff and Akiko Aoyagi in *History of Sesame*, this early mention names sesame among the important crops that were to be planted in the historical Japanese provinces: 'Each feudal domain (kuni) is encouraged to plant millet, barnyard millet, barley, wheat, soybeans, adzuki beans and sesame seeds.'

If you arrive on Shodoshima by ferry across the Seto Inland Sea from Takamatsu, no doubt you will immediately smell something incredible wafting through the air and wonder, what is cooking? Or perhaps you won't even be near the port, but climbing a mountain to get a view of all the islands, making sure not to disturb the monkeys. But, even all the way up here, you will catch a scent on the breeze of the unmistakable toasty, nutty aroma of sesame. In fact, wherever you go on the island, it envelops you immediately. It's coming from the Kadoya Sesame Mills, which have been making sesame products here since 1858.

It is interesting to note that Japan's own sesame seed production has almost disappeared. As a beloved and essential ingredient, some of the oldest sesame manufacturers in the country, who became established before the end of the Edo period and the beginning of the Meiji period, are still going strong thanks to imported seeds. Iwai Sesame was founded in 1857 in Chiba (they moved to Yokohama in 1898 to be closer to the port to better handle sesame shipments); Kadoya, right by Shodo Island's busiest port, Tonosho, was founded in 1858; and Kuki began in 1886 in Mie prefecture with a machine acquired from the British. However, 99.9 per cent of the sesame seeds they turn into oil and paste for Japanese cooking come from abroad.

Wadaman, a 130-year-old sesame company in Osaka, asked themselves what they could do about Japan's domestic harvest ratio being less than 0.1 per cent. The company decided they would encourage local production of sesame in Japan. They still use imported sesame seeds, but they have their own sesame crops in Nara prefecture and also help spread knowledge of sesame cultivation. They work with chemical-free farmers in about 20 districts in Japan, in areas such as Kagoshima, Shimane, Hyogo and Toyama. They even encourage people to grow their own sesame and supply seeds for planting.

MIRACULOUS WILD SESAME

Special mention should also be given to egoma (荏胡麻), a variety of perilla seed (distinct, however from shiso) that is known as 'wild sesame'. Egoma hails from India and China but has been present in Japanese lands for many thousands of years, possibly up to 10,000 years. Its oil was even used to fuel lanterns in Japan's medieval Heian period (794–1185).

Today it's not as widely known or consumed, other than in small pockets here and there, but is increasingly appreciated for its many health and environmental benefits: as the perilla plants mature, they let off an aroma that repels insects and even animals such as wild boars, so has become an important crop to encourage organic farming.

A few years ago I visited a communal egoma field in Chino, Nagano. The local community decided to grow their plants together because it is such back-breaking work to harvest the tiny seeds – they make an excellent and very expensive oil that is highly prized for its nutritional properties. It's extremely rich in important omega 3 fatty acids – just one teaspoon of egoma oil contains the same amount of omega 3 fatty acids as three sardines. In fact, egoma is sometimes known as 'the fish of the fields' and also has the nickname *juunen*, which means 'ten years' – because it's thought that consuming egoma oil will add ten years to your life.

Luckily, there are many delicious ways to add egoma oil to your dishes, if you can find it. First and foremost, it shouldn't be cooked if you want to retain all the health properties. Just drizzle it on salads, tofu, grilled fish or meat, as you would a really good freshly pressed extra virgin olive oil. Or grind in a mortar with some sugar, a splash of water and a touch of soy sauce to make a luxurious, nutty 'butter' to spread on toast or spoon over mochi.

TYPES OF SESAME

Sesame seeds (irigoma, いりごま)

There are three main colours of sesame seeds found in Japan: white, black and gold. **White sesame** is the most mild; **gold sesame** has a stronger aroma and is the favourite for furikake and sauces such as gomaae (page 210); **black sesame** has a nuttier flavour and dark colour and is often used in sweets.

Toasting the seeds gives them a stronger flavour and is best for Japanese dishes. They can burn easily, so you need to keep them moving in the pan. Because they also pop a little, there is a Japanese pan specifically for toasting sesame seeds, called a kotobuki – it has a little mesh net that clips over the top so you can shake the seeds easily without any popping out.

Sesame paste (neri goma, 練りごま)

If you cannot get Japanese sesame paste, Chinese sesame paste is a closer match than tahini. If you do have to use tahini, try to find unhulled tahini, meaning the whole husk is used, so it has a darker colour and a slightly more bitter and robust flavour than regular tahini and is more similar to the Japanese sesame paste.

Of course, you can always put in a bit of elbow grease and grind your own toasted sesame seeds to make neri goma. Traditionally, you would use a suribachi to do this – it's a bit like a mortar and pestle. The suribachi bowl is ceramic with grooves carved into it and the pestle is always wooden. You might find that the oil separates in jars of sesame paste; that's quite normal, just give it a good stir before using.

Sesame oil (goma abura ごま油)

Japanese roasted sesame oil has a wonderful caramel colour and deliciously deep and nutty flavour, because the seeds have been roasted before being pressed. It is more expensive than Chinese sesame oil or other similar oils but I think you'll agree with me that it's worth it. Roasted sesame oil is best for flavouring a dish and I usually add it towards the end of cooking or as a finishing oil – sometimes it's the only condiment you need. Sesame oil is long lasting and doesn't oxidise as easily as other oils when it's kept well, such as in a cool, dark place, not by the stovetop.

SESAME OIL
SURIBACHI
BLACK SESAME
BLACK SESAME
PASTE
TOASTED SESAME
SESAME PASTE
TOASTED
SESAME OIL
436 ml

たたききゅうり

SMASHED CUCUMBER SALAD

TATAKI KYURI

'Tataki' comes from the word for pound or smash (yes, even tuna tataki, page 43, shares this same name, although for a less obvious reason). This is a great summer side dish – it is so refreshing and takes barely any time to make. The smashing of the cucumber is also pretty satisfying: just don't overdo it!

SERVES 2–4

1 long cucumber
½ teaspoon toasted sesame seeds
finely chopped chives; garlic chives or shiso; chopped umeboshi (pickled plum), to serve (optional)

DRESSING

2 cm (¾ in) knob of ginger
1 garlic clove
1 teaspoon soy sauce
1 teaspoon sesame oil
2 teaspoons rice vinegar
pinch of salt

For the dressing, grate the ginger and garlic on an oroshigane grater or microplane into a bowl. Mix in the rest of the dressing ingredients and taste – if you like, add a bit more salt or acidity.

Smash the cucumber all over with a rolling pin or other heavy object until you just break the skin. Chop into bite-sized pieces (about 2 cm/¾ in) and toss with the dressing.

Scatter with the sesame seeds and any of the other optional additions you would like.

胡麻和え

AVOCADO WITH SESAME DRESSING

AVOCADO NO GOMA-AE

This sesame sauce is one of the classics of Japanese home cooking, and can be used to dress up any simply blanched or raw vegetables. My grandmother would usually do this with spinach (if you want to try that, follow the spinach preparation for shiraee, page 212). It's also delicious with blanched broccoli, green beans, asparagus, raw grated carrots and even non-Japanese produce such as avocado. I also love this on a chilled wobbly block of tofu.

For the gomaae, make sure you're using toasted sesame seeds. If, by chance, you've got raw sesame seeds, you'll need to toast them to a hazelnut-brown colour first.

While the gomaae can be made in advance, you want to dice and dress the avocado right before serving.

SERVES 2

1 avocado, peeled and diced

GOMAAE

1 tablespoon toasted sesame seeds

1 teaspoon soy sauce

1 teaspoon sesame oil

pinch of sugar

To make the gomaae, grind the sesame seeds with a suribachi or mortar and pestle to release their flavour. I like them just a little bit ground – lightly crushed and a bit powdery. Add the soy sauce, sesame oil and sugar.

Taste to check the flavours – the sugar is to counter the saltiness and shouldn't overpower the sauce.

Pour over the diced avocado, mix gently to coat and serve immediately.

ほうれん草の白和え

SPINACH WITH TOFU, MISO & SESAME

HORENSOU NO SHIRA-AE

Like gomaae (page 210), this is usually served as a small side dish as part of a traditional *ichiju-sansai* – 'one soup, three dishes'. This dish was often on our table as one of the many side dishes my obaachan would prepare for us. It's a luscious, creamy sauce made with silken tofu, miso and sesame that can be used to dress any favourite vegetable – spinach is a classic, but it's also great with green beans, asparagus, even mushrooms. Lightly blanch or sauté the vegetables first and then toss them in this sauce. I particularly love this with broccoli – including the stems and leaves, not just the florets.

My mother makes this with young English spinach with pink roots, trimming them to keep as much of the pink stems as possible – this is the most nutritious, iron-rich part of the spinach. It's also a way to use as much of the vegetable as possible – so often we throw away the most nutritious parts of fruits and vegetables (the skins, for example).

In shojin ryori, Buddhist temple cuisine, where this dish originated, not wasting food is an important, thoughtful part of any recipe.

SERVES 4

400 g (14 oz) English spinach
1 tablespoon toasted sesame seeds
120 g (4½ oz) silken tofu
1 teaspoon sugar
1 teaspoon soy sauce
1 teaspoon white miso

Wash the spinach really well. If you've got young bunches, keep them attached at the root but make sure to get all the dirt out from around the root. Trim as much of the root as possible while keeping the bunch intact, especially the pink part of the stem.

Blanch the spinach in boiling water until just wilted – 1 minute should do it – then plunge it into cold water. Drain very well and squeeze out all the excess moisture. Cut into sections about 4 cm (1½ in) long.

Grind the sesame seeds with a suribachi or mortar and pestle to release their flavour. I like them just a little bit ground – lightly crushed and a bit powdery.

Add the tofu, sugar, soy sauce and miso to the suribachi and grind to a smooth sauce – it doesn't take much, as the silken tofu instantly turns to a cream.

Toss the spinach through the sauce to serve. This will keep in the fridge for 2–3 days.

キャベツのソテー

STIR-FRIED SESAME CABBAGE

KYABETSU NO SOTE

This is perhaps my favourite way to eat cabbage, ever (and there are a lot of good ways to eat cabbage). It's something quick and delicious my mother makes when there's nothing in the fridge. She has always been very good at making dinner materialise out of nowhere.

This simple combination of salt, sesame oil and sesame seeds on vegetables is always a winner, so if you don't even have cabbage, on one of those sad days when the fridge is empty, this is also great with julienned carrots, mung beans, spinach or any leafy greens that cook quickly. Instead of stir-frying, you can also steam or blanch the vegetables – in this case I would go with green beans, broccoli, edamame or bok choy, just to give you a few ideas.

SERVES 4

500 g (1 lb 2 oz) cabbage
2 tablespoons sesame oil
pinch of salt
1–2 teaspoons toasted sesame seeds

Chop the cabbage roughly into bite-sized squares.

Heat half the sesame oil in a frying pan over medium heat. Cook the cabbage, tossing with the salt, for about 5 minutes until softened and browned here and there.

Pile into a bowl and sprinkle with sesame seeds and the rest of the sesame oil to serve.

すったてうどん

UDON IN CHILLED SESAME SAUCE

SUTTATE UDON

This little-known dish comes from the Kawajima area in the prefecture of Saitama, just north of Tokyo, where sesame and wheat abound. It was originally a peasant dish that was almost lost – known only to farmers, rarely written about or replicated outside of the area. Now, however, local chefs are keeping the tradition alive for this summertime dish. The soft noodles are easy to eat when your body is exhausted from the heat; they are served chilled as a refreshing, uplifting meal.

The sauce is what makes this dish special and it is often prepared – pounded in a suribachi – right at the table. Some restaurants in Kawajima even serve the bowl of fresh sesame seeds for diners to grind themselves. To the ground seeds are added miso, cucumbers, spring onion and shiso leaves (the mashing of the vegetables is what gives the dish its name: *suritate* means 'freshly mashed'). The sauce is then loosened with dashi or water until it is the perfect dipping consistency.

I have made this recipe for one person, as I think of this as my ideal meal for one, where the bowl of sauce is made at the table and the suribachi or mortar becomes the noodle-dipping bowl. If you are serving more people and have a large suribachi, simply multiply the quantities and pour the sauce into a separate bowl for each diner.

SERVES 1

150 g (5½ oz) fresh udon noodles
ice cubes (optional)
30 g (¼ cup) toasted sesame seeds
1 spring onion, finely chopped
¼ long cucumber, thinly sliced
shiso leaf, finely sliced (optional)
1 tablespoon miso
125 ml (½ cup) chilled dashi (pages 108–9) or water

Boil the noodles according to the packet instructions – a few minutes is usually enough for fresh noodles. Drain and rinse immediately in cold water to cool them down and give them a bit of bounce. Put in a bowl and add a handful of ice cubes to keep them chilled.

Place the sesame seeds in a suribachi or mortar and lightly grind until they are partially broken up and fragrant. Add the spring onion, cucumber and shiso leaf, bashing them to break them up slightly.

Add the miso and some of the dashi, stirring to loosen the miso and combine the sauce. Continue to pound and stir, while adding as much dashi or water as you like to get a dipping-sauce consistency.

On particularly hot days you might add ice cubes to the sauce too. To eat, dip the noodles into the sauce and don't be afraid to enjoy with great slurping!

餃子

GYOZA WITH SESAME SAUCE

I grew up in Beijing. I spent the most important years of my adolescence there, from age 11 to 18, and the food I was exposed to at that impressionable time had a deep impact on my passion for cooking. We had a Chinese cook, as did many expatriate diplomatic families in the 1990s, who did all the food shopping at the market and arrived in the afternoon to cook dinner five nights a week.

Mr Zhang was an incredibly sweet man, with a wide smile on his face always. I loved coming home from school to discover he was making jiaozi, not only because we would get to eat them, but because I could help make them, too. In my life, I have definitely eaten more jiaozi than gyoza (the Japanese pronunciation of the same Chinese characters). This is perhaps because living in Beijing contributed to my preference for the northern Chinese tradition of eating dumplings boiled rather than fried, and dipped only in vinegar rather than soy sauce. Nonetheless, I am not one to ever say no to a dumpling, whether boiled or fried, and fried gyoza happen to be the favourite of the rest of my family.

You can definitely use pre-made dumpling wrappers, instead of making the dough yourself, but, where I live, I find it's easier than hunting around for them. They are pretty quick to make and the dough is softer and less dry than the bought ones, meaning these cook quickly and more evenly.

MAKES about 50

- **300 g (10½ oz) minced pork with a good fat content**
- **1 teaspoon soy sauce**
- **1 teaspoon sake**
- **1 teaspoon sesame oil, plus extra for greasing**
- **2–3 spring onions (scallions), very finely chopped**
- **2–3 cm (1 in) knob of ginger, peeled and grated**
- **1 teaspoon salt**
- **300 g (10½ oz) napa cabbage, finely chopped**
- **potato starch or plain (all-purpose) flour, for dusting**

SESAME SAUCE

- **1 teaspoon soy sauce**
- **1 teaspoon rice vinegar**
- **1 teaspoon sesame paste**
- **1 teaspoon sesame oil**

WRAPPERS

- **300 g (2 cups) plain (all-purpose) flour**
- **150 ml (5 fl oz) just-boiled water**
- **potato starch or plain (all-purpose) flour, for dusting**

Mix together the pork, soy sauce, sake, sesame oil, spring onions, ginger and ½ teaspoon of the salt with your hands until well incorporated. If you have time, leave this for a few hours – overnight even – for the flavours to mingle.

Put the cabbage in a bowl, toss with ½ teaspoon salt and leave for 15 minutes to remove some of the water. Squeeze out the cabbage in a sieve.

Stir together the sesame sauce ingredients until smooth. If necessary, loosen with a dash of water. Set aside.

To make the wrappers, put the flour in a bowl. Boil some water and let it cool for a few minutes before measuring out. Use chopsticks to mix the water into the flour until it looks a bit shaggy. Now knead with your hands – it should come together quite quickly into a very soft, smooth dough. Cover and leave to rest for 15 minutes.

On a chopping board, flatten the dough into a disc. Poke a hole in the middle and widen to a ring about 3 fingers in diameter. Cut pieces from this, rolling into little cherry-sized balls (they should each weigh about 10 g/¼ oz). Flatten and roll out from the centre in all directions until the wrapper fits your palm. If you need, dust the board with potato starch. Keep going until you have made 50 wrappers.

When you are ready to stuff the dumplings, mix the drained cabbage into the pork filling.

Continued ›

Dust a board with potato starch and fill a small bowl with water. Place a heaped teaspoon of filling in the centre of each wrapper. If you need to, dip your finger in the water and run it around the edge of the wrapper. Fold the wrapper in half, pinching from the edge, folding and pinching every centimetre or so to make a crimped pattern and seal the dumpling. Place each dumpling on the floured board.

To cook the dumplings, place them in a greased frying pan, stacked close together over medium heat. Pour in 2 tablespoons water and cover with a tight-fitting lid; do not touch or move the dumplings now. Cook for 6 minutes and then check – the dough should look shiny and a bit translucent, rather than opaque. If not, put the lid back on (add another drop of water, if necessary) and cook for a further minute.

Remove the lid and cook briefly until any excess moisture has evaporated – the dumplings should be crisp and browned slightly on the bottom. Flip them onto a plate with a spatula and serve with the sesame sauce.

しゃぶしゃぶ

SHABU SHABU

This delicious hot pot is a fun dish to make when you have a table full of people – it's all about conviviality. It's usually cooked in the middle of the table on a portable gas stove. If that's not possible for you, cook everything in the pot and serve deep bowls of broth with a bit of every ingredient added to each bowl.

The base of the stew is a simple dashi broth, served with a platter of raw ingredients – such as napa cabbage, Japanese mushrooms, noodles, broccoli, carrot, squares of tofu, and thin slices of beef or pork (vegetarians can leave these out). You cook these in the broth, then pull them out and dip them into individual bowls of sauces, usually both ponzu and sesame sauce. My favourite is always the sesame sauce. You can add ponzu too (page 43).

Shabu shabu was apparently invented in Osaka in 1952, at a restaurant called Suehiro, as a lighter version of Tokyo-style sukiyaki. It immediately became popular and is now found all over the country and in many variations, including regional and seasonal.

Use pork loin, belly or shoulder, or beef if you prefer. The most important thing is for the meat to be sliced as thinly as possible. If you can't buy it already paper thin (as you can in Japan), firm it up in the freezer for 30 minutes before slicing with a very sharp knife.

SERVES 4

5 cm (2 in) piece of daikon, thinly sliced
¼ carrot, thinly sliced
300 g (10½ oz) pork or beef loin, thinly sliced
4 shiitake mushrooms
200 g (7 oz) napa cabbage, roughly chopped
100 g (3½ oz) enoki mushrooms, trimmed, separated into bunches of 4
150 g (5½ oz) firm tofu, sliced
1 spring onion (scallion), finely chopped
50 g (1¾ oz) mung bean sprouts
small bunch of garlic chives
steamed rice (page 36), to serve
ponzu sauce (page 43, optional)

BROTH

2 litres (8 cups) kombu dashi (page 108)
125 ml (½ cup) sake

SESAME SAUCE

3 tablespoons sesame paste
1½ tablespoons soy sauce
2 teaspoons rice vinegar
2 teaspoons sugar

For the broth, combine the dashi and sake in a large pot and bring to a simmer. Cook for 2–3 minutes and then keep warm.

For the sesame sauce, whisk together all the ingredients, adding about 125 ml (½ cup) of the broth. Whisk until smooth – if it's too thick, add a little more broth. Place in small bowls for each guest.

Arrange all the raw ingredients on a platter and give everyone a bowl of freshly steamed rice.

To serve, place the hot pot in the middle of the table and bring to a gentle simmer. To the broth, add the longer-cooking foods first, such as the daikon, carrot, meat, cabbage, and then finally the rest, or what fits.

As the food is ready, pick it out – use a pair of communal chopsticks that are just for distributing food from the hot pot and not for eating with. Dip in the sesame sauce before eating, or alternate between the rich sesame and the fresh ponzu sauces.

胡麻豆腐

SESAME 'TOFU'

GOMA DOFU

This dish was supposedly created over 1200 years ago by Zen Buddhist monks, whose strict cuisine, shojin ryori, is vegan. Sesame is an important ingredient as it is so rich in nutrients and particularly high in protein (it's called the 'meat of the fields' in Japan).

Goma dofu means 'sesame tofu', but this isn't technically a tofu: it is a sort of pudding made with sesame seeds or paste and kuzu starch, which comes from the roots of a very special Japanese mountain plant. Kuzu is a powerful thickener that works like many other starches (arrowroot or tapioca starch is similar), for thickening sauces, making puddings and even making a special tea (page 242) that is considered a home remedy for colds.

In Buddhist temple cuisine this dish is made from whole toasted sesame seeds that must be painstakingly ground in a suribachi until incredibly smooth (this can take one person an hour to do, but it is part of the monks' spiritual training, requiring patience and dedication). Here, sesame paste makes things a little bit easier. Look for toasted Japanese or Chinese sesame paste, or use unhulled tahini, which has a darker colour.

Goma dofu is a very popular summertime dish – refreshing and cooling, much like jelly. Since it has a neutral flavour, you can even make it into a dessert by dressing with brown sugar syrup or maple syrup. It is traditionally served with soy sauce and wasabi (one of the ultimate condiments, if you ask me, but it must be freshly grated, rather than out of a tube, for the real-deal experience). I like freshly grated ginger here, too, or the delicious vinegar-miso dressing for nuta (page 188).

This recipe is inspired by NHK World-Japan's *Nun's Cookbook* – a fascinating series that you can watch on YouTube. It highlights temple recipes cooked by the nuns of Otowasan Kannon-ji Temple in Nara.

SERVES 4

30 g (1 oz) kuzu starch
60 g (2 oz) toasted sesame paste
pinch of salt
250 ml (1 cup) water
freshly grated ginger or wasabi and soy sauce, to serve

Before you start, find an appropriate tray or container to use as a mould. I use a small baking dish about 14 x 10 cm (6 x 4 in). Half-fill it with water and then tip out the water so it remains wet.

Put the kuzu starch, sesame paste, salt and water in a small saucepan and whisk until smooth. Place over low heat and whisk slowly but continuously until it starts to thicken. Now whisk faster and, once it gets really thick, keep whisking for an extra minute. Pour into the mould.

Place baking paper or plastic wrap directly on top of the goma dofu to stop it drying out. Put in the fridge and leave to set and cool completely.

Once set, tip out onto a board and slice into 4 pieces. Serve with grated ginger or wasabi and a splash of soy sauce.

精進料理の真髄

Japan's no-waste temple cuisine

Shojin ryori (精進料理) is a plant-based temple cuisine associated with Zen Buddhism that was developed in Kyoto in the 13th century. *Shojin* can be interpreted as 'the desire to improve yourself' or 'making effort to strive for limitless perfection'. *Ryori* means, quite simply, 'cuisine'.

The act of preparing shojin ryori itself is a part of the Buddhist practice, the pursuit of enlightenment. It is the oldest codified cuisine in the country, having its origins in the sixth century, when Chinese and Korean monks brought Buddhism to Japan.

Over the centuries the food developed into its own Japanese style, and a manual, *Tenzo Kyōkun* (典座教訓), *Instructions for the Cook*, was written in 1237 by Eihei Dogen, founder of the Zen sect of Buddhism. It is much more than just a cooking manual: '*Instructions for the Cook* are instructions for life,' he wrote. It describes not only what to prepare and how to serve it, but also what kind of monk is suitable to be a tenzo (head cook), and the importance of the cook's mindfulness and attitude. With a clear mind, the act of preparing ingredients is no different from a Buddhist awakening, Dogen suggests.

Non-violence is one of the most important beliefs of Buddhism. Buddha is said to have said, 'the eating of meat extinguishes the seed of compassion'. As consuming meat, along with alcohol (and pungent alliums such as garlic and onion, which excite the body), is strictly prohibited in shojin ryori, vegetables, soybeans and nuts make up the main ingredients. Sesame, tofu and walnuts, for example, became popular and spread throughout Japan, thanks to shojin ryori.

Hyper-seasonality, the use of only local ingredients, paying attention to nature, nutritional balance and sustenance are all part of this traditional cuisine. Other important aspects include treating the ingredients with respect, being grateful for what is available, and not wasting anything (even skins, roots and leaves that might otherwise be discarded), or 'mottainai'.

Mottainai is an expression in Japanese that means 'regret at the full value of something not being put to good use' and it is not limited to food preparation or the dinner table.

The Buddhologist Kato Totsudo wrote an essay in 1934 that describes mottainai as a 'core Japanese personality trait'. You will find this spirit in many areas of everyday life, from repair shops to the complex recycling system, even toy hospitals (Japan has hundreds of these) that fix old toys and encourage children to care for belongings, and the arts — from sashiko stitching to kintsugi, where broken ceramic wares are repaired with precious gold dust and urushi lacquer.

Chef Daisuke Nomura, who was born into a shojin ryori restaurant family and now runs his own, Sougo in Tokyo, passes on the philosophy of living in harmony with nature and respecting all living things through his Buddhist cuisine, saying: 'For us to survive, we receive the lives of other things, so we must not waste them.' ●

黒ごまシフォンケーキ

BLACK SESAME CHIFFON CAKE

KUROGOMA SHIFON KEIKI

My dear friend Junko Mizoguchi, a talented baker, is famous for her chiffon cake. She makes it for every birthday party and gathering and wows everyone with its impossibly fluffy texture. She always serves it plain, just as it is. It's so good it needs no adornments.

Before she moved back to Japan, she gifted me her chiffon cake tin and her recipe to go with it. We made her cake together and she showed me the trick for making sure it doesn't sink after baking – she turned it upside down like a panettone and cooled it on top of a wine bottle!

I have always had a soft spot for black sesame desserts, and I decided to alter her recipe in just one small way – with some black sesame paste. The result is still her famously fluffy cake but with a hint of nuttiness and a distinctive Totoro-grey colour. Look for black sesame paste with no added salt – or forgo the salt in the recipe. Add some hand-ground black sesame seeds if you would like this speckled. Either way, it is a delight.

MAKES 1 cake

6 eggs
pinch of salt
130 g (4½ oz) sugar
90 ml (3 fl oz) water
60 ml (¼ cup) olive oil
120 g (about 1 cup) plain (all-purpose) flour
1 teaspoon baking powder
35 g (1¼ oz) black sesame paste

Heat the oven to 170°C (340°F). Carefully separate the eggs (note, you will end up with a spare yolk). Place 5 yolks in a bowl with the salt and half the sugar and beat with electric beaters until pale, fluffy and doubled in volume. Set aside.

Whip the egg whites in a clean, dry bowl with no trace of grease. Once they are very frothy, start adding the rest of the sugar, a spoonful at a time, whipping constantly until you have a glossy, thick meringue. The moment it is done is the moment when you can tilt the bowl and the meringue doesn't slide or move at all. Stop now.

Add the water and olive oil to the yolk mixture and beat well. Sift together the flour and baking powder and add to the yolk mixture, folding in with a spatula until no flour is visible and there are no lumps. Gradually fold in the egg whites, one third at a time, until you have a smooth, fluffy mixture.

Pour into a dry 20 cm (8 in) chiffon cake tin – do not grease at all! The cake rises by clinging to the side of the tin. Bake on the middle shelf for 35–40 minutes, or until springy on top.

Let the cake cool upside-down by slipping it over the top of a wine bottle – you can also cool it upside down on a rack, if it didn't rise over the top of the tin. Run a palette knife around the edge of the tin to release the cake and turn out.

This keeps well in an airtight container or covered in plastic wrap, for 3 days at room temperature.

茶

TEA

'Tea is the elixir of life.'

EISAI, ZEN MONK AND AUTHOR OF *KISSA YOJOKI*, 1211

The first records of tea-drinking in Japan date back to the eighth century, when Buddhist monks, returning to Japan from China, brought back tea from the *Camellia sinensis* plant. Kukai (774–835) and Saicho (767–822) had become friends after a chance meeting in Fukuoka, while they waited for the seas to calm to allow their travel to China. They were going to study religion and later became founders of the Shingon and Tendai schools of Buddhism, respectively; they also just happened to bring back the first tea to Japan – both for drinking and for planting. Little did they know what an enormous influence this would have on all of Japanese culture.

About ten years later, in 815, Emperor Saga became the first Emperor to drink tea. Until then, it had been seen as a medicinal drink and part of the monks' Buddhist practice. The Emperor loved it so much that he encouraged tea planting. He was a great supporter of Kukai, also helping him establish his school of Buddhism at Toji Temple in current day Kyoto, where he planted the first tea seeds in Japan. However, after Emperor Saga's death in 842, it seems tea-drinking fell out of favour in noble circles, and remained simply a practice within temple walls (mainly to help the monks stay awake while meditating). Otherwise, it was largely forgotten.

It wasn't until over 300 years later that another Buddhist monk, Eisai, made tea-drinking popular again. He, too, planted seeds after a trip to China, in 1191, first in Kyushu and then Kyoto. He also gave seeds to another monk, Myoe, of the Kozan-ji temple in Kyoto, who planted them in the town of Uji, near the then-capital, Kyoto. Within a couple of centuries, Uji's tea became so well known it was termed *honcha* (本茶), 'real tea'. It is still famous today and at the centre of Japan's prestigious matcha production.

In 1211 Eisai wrote the *Kissa Yojoki*, 喫茶養生記, the 'Treatise of drinking tea for health', the first of its kind. It opens with the phrase: 'Tea is the most wonderful medicine for nourishing one's health; it is the elixir of life.' It goes on to describe how to grow tea and process the leaves, as well as giving a thorough explanation of the drink's health benefits.

This treatise is also what introduced tea-drinking to the samurai class, when Eisai demonstrated his point on the hungover shogun Minamoto no Sanetomo. Not only did tea prove a useful hangover cure, but, just as for the meditating monks, the caffeine in matcha provided long-lasting energy (it is notably absorbed by the body much more slowly than coffee). It became an important tool for samurai, helping them stay alert and focused before going into battle, but tea remained a beverage that was mainly enjoyed by the privileged.

It was only through the work of tea master Sen no Rikyu (1522–1591) that tea eventually became available to commoners. Rikyu developed the art of the tea ceremony under his master (and matcha fan), the feudal lord Toyotomi Hideyoshi. The ceremony became an important cultural practice in Japan around this time. Preparation of tea followed a strict set of rules, using specific utensils in a specific order, and was practised as a form of political diplomacy (hence the need for rulers to have an informed, and loyal, tea master).

Special tea huts and rooms were constructed for performing the tea ceremonies, where everything from the utensils and the style and colour of the teaware were carefully chosen to enhance the experience. Wabicha (like *wabi-sabi*, 侘び寂び, or the 'appreciation of the imperfect, impermanent and incomplete') refers to the use of tea ceremony objects that are intentionally flawed – this aesthetic was already being applied in the 15th century.

The young Florentine merchant, Francesco Carletti, who visited Japan in 1597–98, was surprised at how revered tea was. In his posthumously published travel account, *Ragionamenti*, he described an unusual conservation method of the ground tea (matcha), using ancient vases that were brought from Southeast Asia: 'In the morning, before we set foot on the land, ministers of justice came by command of the governor of that region, so as to search among all the sailors, passengers and merchants for certain earthenware vases that often are brought there from the Philippine Islands and other places in that sea. By order of Japan, these must, under pain of death, be showed by anyone who has them, as the King wishes to buy them all. Who ever would believe it? Those vases often are worth five, six, or ten thousand s*cudi* each, though ordinarily one would not say that they were worth a *giulio* [a coin of little value] and the reason is that they have the property of preserving unspoiled – and for nine, ten and twenty years – a certain leaf called cha.'

To give you an idea of what five or ten thousand *scudi* would have been worth at the time, imagine five to ten Titian paintings: the artist was paid 1000 *scudi* for each portrait he painted of King Philip II of Spain, his most important patron.

Carletti continues: 'It seems a superstition, and yet it is true, that it is preserved well only in the aforesaid vases made simply of a clay that has this virtue. But they are very few and very well known to those people, who recognise them by certain signs and characters in antique lettering, which show them to be of ancient manufacture. They are not to be found today except as they were made many hundreds of years ago and are brought from the kingdoms of Cambodia and of Siam and Cochin China and from the islands, Philippine and other, of that sea… Many merchants have become rich on them. The king of this Japan and all the other princes of the reign have an infinite number of these vases, which they regard as their principal treasure, esteeming them more than anything else of value.'

The vases that Carletti documented are called *chigusa* (literally 'thousand grasses', meaning myriad things). These glazed, stoneware vases were made in southern China around the 12th to 13th centuries as ordinary storage jars, but by the 16th century had become antique collectibles that were prized by tea connoisseurs. Diaries kept by tea masters confirm the extraordinary high status of these cherished objects. Their role in the tea ceremony was to preserve the freshly harvested spring tea leaves until autumn; the jars could perfectly maintain the quality of the leaves, while allowing the flavour to ripen. Proud owners of these priceless vessels would sign their names on the bottom of the jars, leaving their imprint on their favourite tea accessories.

Carletti goes on to describe how the tea is served and used, describing, in particular, the medicinal effects of matcha: 'From its leaves they make a powder that they then mix with hot water – which they continually have on the fire for this purpose, in an iron cauldron – and then drink it daily, more as a medicine than for its taste. It has a somewhat bitter flavour, so that one then washes out the mouth. Upon those who take it good and flavoursome, it produces a very good effect and relieves the stomach weakness because of its warmth. It marvellously assists digestion and is especially excellent for lightening and impeding the fumes that rise to the head. And, for that reason, it customarily is drunk immediately after the midday meal, when one feels full of too much wine: and drinking it after supper brings on sleep. In sum, the uses of drinking this cha are so many that one never enters a house without being offered it in a friendly way, out of good manners, as a matter of custom to honour the guest.'

From the Edo period (1603–1868) onwards, the popularity of tea grew enormously, in all levels of society. Restaurants served tea, and tea shops opened. Many teas were still a luxury that only the most wealthy could afford, while the common people, particularly in the countryside, drank bancha.

Like so many Japanese-made foods and arts that came about during this period of self-isolation, new ways of processing teas were explored. It is during this period that sencha (1738) and gyokuro (1835) teas were created; it's also when tea began to be widely distributed and sold throughout Japan, expanding the areas of production, before being exported too.

HOJICHA
POWDER
SENCHA
HOJICHA
GENMAICHA
PREMIUM
MATCHA
AKAMATSUCHA
SOBA CHA
CULINARY
GRADE MATCHA

TYPES OF JAPANESE TEA

The Japanese word for tea is cha, 茶, and it is often referred to with the honorific 'o' in front of it: ocha. Green, black and oolong tea are all made from the *Camellia sinensis* plant, which is native to south-western China.

The earliest teas in Japan were known as 'brick tea' or **dancha**, meaning a hard block of well-pressed tea leaves – leaves were scraped from the block and put into boiling water. In the 12th century Eisai introduced a new kind of tea preparation he had learned in China called **chanoyu** (literally 'tea's hot water', which later came to mean 'the way of tea'). The leaves were first ground to a powder before adding to the water and the drink was used to help priests stay awake when meditating. Although the practice disappeared in China, this powdered form of tea became **matcha** and was refined in Japanese culture.

Matcha 抹茶

Uji is a small village to the south of Kyoto that is synonymous with matcha. In the late 12th century the first tea bushes were planted here by the monk Myoe. The location is important in the history of tea, because it was close to Kyoto, the capital at the time, but had a more suitable climate for tea-producing. Uji had rich soil, abundant fresh water and a river that kept the village under mist in the cooler months. It quickly became known for its high-quality tea and the tea was referred to as 'Ujicha'.

In the 14th century a hand-cranked stone mill (ishi usu) for grinding tea leaves into a fine powder replaced the previous wooden grinder (known as a yagen). The quality and appreciation for this tea grew, and by the mid-1500s, the word 'matcha' – referencing the powder created by 'rubbing' or grinding – appears in a Japanese dictionary.

For centuries before this, matcha had been consumed primarily as a medicinal drink rather than for pleasure, and many modern studies have confirmed that the ancient knowledge and instincts about its health benefits were correct – it can help strengthen the immune system, lower blood pressure and cholesterol, and is believed to have anti-aging and anti-cancer properties, to name a few.

Matcha is made by stone-grinding dried, steamed tea leaves (called tencha) into a very fine powder. The leaves for matcha are shaded from the sun for a few weeks before harvest – since harvest is in May, this usually happens by mid-April – which deepens their colour as it increases chlorophyll and decreases tannins, leading to a sweeter flavour. The technique was developed in 16th century Uji and, for centuries, was only permitted in Uji.

The highest grade premium matcha is bright green and made with the youngest, most tender and vibrant leaves, giving it a fresh, grassy, sweet umami flavour. Lower grade matcha powders (like the one marked 'culinary grade') will be duller olive green because they are made from older, tougher leaves, or weren't shaded properly, and will taste more bitter. Take this into account when using matcha to drink or use in any recipes.

Even though these are marked for culinary use, I personally use a higher grade matcha for everything – I love the colour and flavour. Even good-quality matcha ages and oxidises, turning duller in colour and losing flavour.

Matcha tea has two different consistencies: **usucha**, which is a regular matcha; and **koicha**, which is very thick, intense and soupy – only the highest quality matcha is suitable for this kind of beverage.

Sencha 煎茶

Meaning 'boiled tea', sencha was developed in the 1700s, when a Uji tea-grower first steamed the young tender leaves and then rolled them and dried them. It became hugely popular – it was a much more carefree way to brew tea than the stricter tea ceremony techniques people had been accustomed to. To this day, sencha represents about 80 per cent of all Japanese tea. This is a special tea to serve to guests; it should be brewed with water no hotter than 80°C (176°F) and steeped for one minute.

There is a higher grade version of this rolled tea called **gyokuro** – the young leaves of the tea trees are shaded, as for matcha, but then rolled like sencha to make a very expensive, premium loose-leaf green tea. There are also countless teas made from the gyokuro off-cuts, and even the leftover dust from processing.

These no-waste teas even have their own categories: for example, the tea made from the stalks trimmed from gyokuro leaves is called **kukicha**; tea made from gyokuro dust is **konacha**; while **mecha** is made from too-small, underdeveloped gyokuro leaves. There is also a tea called **kabusecha**, which is something between gyokuro and sencha – the tea plants are covered with a screen of straw, as for matcha, but only for a few days rather than weeks. They are then steamed and rolled, like gyokuro.

Bancha 番茶

This is an everyday tea, ideal for breakfast, for anytime, for home. It is coarser, more rustic and contains older leaves that are steamed and sun-dried without the painstaking rolling. These tea leaves can simply be added to boiling water.

Hojicha is basically a nutty, roasted bancha, where the green tea is first roasted until golden brown. It was apparently discovered by accident in 1920. The roasting process removes bitterness and caffeine, so this can be enjoyed at all times of the day and night, even at bedtime. It is often drunk as an iced tea in the summer.

Genmaicha is considered another bancha, but it can also be made with kabusecha or sencha leaves, or even have matcha powder added to it. It is also low in caffeine and contains grains of roasted, popped brown rice with a nutty flavour reminiscent of popcorn or rice crackers. Genmaicha has very humble origins, being that brown rice once served as a filler to reduce the price of the tea for the poorest classes. This is one of my personal favourites – nutty, toasty, full flavoured and easy to drink at any time of the day.

Oolong tea ウーロン茶

Oolong is a Chinese tea; Japanese oolong tea is produced in small quantities. Made from the same tree species as green tea, oolong is semi-oxidised or fermented, as opposed to black tea, which is fully fermented, and green tea, which is not fermented at all. Its popularity took off in the 1970s and 80s. Around this time, as carbonated drinks were becoming popular in Japan and people began drinking less tea, one tea company, Ito En, developed oolong tea in a can. It was a hit.

Today you'll find canned oolong tea sold in every restaurant, izakaya, vending machine and konbini in Japan. I mention this mostly as an idea of what to drink with Japanese food other than sake or beer. This is often the main non-alcoholic drink served in Japan with food, and it is just as loved in a chilled version as it is warm.

OTHER TEAS

There are 'teas' made from many things other than leaves: **sobacha** is buckwheat tea; **kobucha** is tea made from kombu; **sakuracha** is made with salt-pickled cherry blossoms for special occasions; and **mugicha** is made from roasted barley and popular as iced tea. Tea can be made also from **akamatsu**, red pine.

HOW TO STORE TEAS

Keep your tea in an airtight container in a cool, dark place. Once opened, be sure to use it and enjoy it at its freshest. If you don't drink tea frequently, you can keep it in the freezer to keep it fresher.

Keep matcha powder in its closed container in a cool, dark place. If you don't use it often (yet), start with matcha in a small container. Once opened, be sure to use it; don't just leave it there waiting for special occasions! The older the tea, the less vibrant its colour and flavour.

Matcha is not only sensitive to light and heat, but also to other odours, so don't keep it with your spices. You can also freeze matcha; let it come to room temperature before using. If it's been frozen, it will be particularly important to sift it before using.

抹茶の点て方

HOW TO MAKE MATCHA TEA

MATCHA NO TATEKATA

A good cup of matcha – bittersweet, rich, grassy and vibrant – envelops you like a blanket. The opaque frothy tea is thicker than any regular cup of tea – you are drinking the whole tea leaf itself, unlike other teas which are an infusion of the leaves. There is nothing like it.

You could – and some have – write an entire book on how to make the perfect matcha tea, but rather than go into the ceremony that surrounds serving it, this is a simple guide to making and enjoying matcha at home.

To make it special, serve it in a bowl rather than a cup. If you like, you could acquire a chasen, a bamboo whisk with very fine tines, for whisking matcha – they are relatively easy to find, not too expensive and are beautiful. You can use a regular metal whisk if you don't have one.

As we've noted, there are different qualities of matcha tea. The highest quality powders have a vibrant green colour; lower grade matcha, or the one labelled 'culinary grade', is more olive green and more bitter, so take this into account. I use the highest grade for everything.

If you prefer a stronger flavour, use the full teaspoon; otherwise, start with half that.

SERVES 1

185 ml (¾ cup) hot water
½–1 teaspoon premium matcha powder

Put the kettle on and boil some water. Ideally, you want it slightly cooled to about 80°C (176°F) when you add it to the tea, so measure out and let it cool for a few minutes before using.

Sift the powder into a tea bowl. Add a tablespoon or so of the hot water and whisk to a smooth paste, making sure there are no dry lumps.

Pour in the rest of the hot water and use your whisk in a zig-zag pattern until you have a slightly frothy surface of fine bubbles and a smooth, delicious matcha.

葛湯

SWEET ARROWROOT TEA

KUZUYU

This comforting, warming drink is considered a traditional Japanese remedy for colds and indigestion, or if you're just feeling under the weather. It is thickened with kuzu starch, which is made from the roots of the resilient Japanese kudzu vine (*Pueraria montana var. lobata*) and has a 2000-year history as a traditional Chinese medicine – a sort of cure-all that can fix everything from muscular pain to hypertension to fevers and even hangovers. Above all, it's known for its usefulness in calming gut issues and as a general antioxidant and anti-inflammatory.

If you don't have kuzu, you can make this with arrowroot (tapioca starch), which might be easier to get and still has some worthy health benefits, mainly for soothing the digestive system.

Kuzu yu can be both sweet and savoury – either will keep you feeling warm on a cold day. Popular additions include black sesame paste, matcha, hojicha, kinako (roast soybean powder), yuzu, cinnamon, honey and, in savoury versions, umeboshi, soy sauce and ginger. Or enjoy it completely plain with just a pinch of salt or a spoonful of sugar.

This is my favourite combination: freshly grated ginger and Okinawan black sugar, which has a deep caramel flavour and is rich in iron. Brown sugar will do too – whatever makes it pleasurable and delicious for you. Because, importantly, feeling good is also part of the role of any comforting pick-me-up.

SERVES 1

2 teaspoons kuzu starch (or arrowroot)
1 tablespoon black or brown sugar
1 teaspoon hojicha powder (optional)
150 ml (5 fl oz) water
pinch of grated ginger

Put the kuzu, sugar, hojicha and water in a small pan and mix together thoroughly before turning on the heat. Bring to the boil, stirring continuously until it thickens and turns transparent – this will happen very quickly as the kuzu is a powerful thickening agent. Spoon into a cup or bowl, top with the ginger and enjoy immediately.

ロイヤルミルクティー

ROYAL MILK TEA

Every train station platform, every vending machine, every konbini (convenience store) or cafe in Japan has some form of hot or chilled Royal milk tea. In supermarkets you'll also find it in powder form, where you can add a sachet to boiling water and get this instant cup of milky tea. But, before I ever tasted it from a can or sachet, my mother would prepare it for me on the stove, especially if I was feeling under the weather. Since then, it has always been my automatic response when someone I love doesn't feel well – *Do you want a milk tea?*

My children love it too, and noticed that it features in their favourite Japanese animation, *Ponyo*: After a storm cuts off all the power, the first thing Sosuke's mother does is make Sosuke and his new, magical friend, Ponyo, cups of milk tea with honey.

There are several stories as to how Royal milk tea became such an iconic drink in Japan: some say it was a great marketing campaign by Lipton tea for a new brand that arrived on the Japanese market in 1965; some have it invented by a Japanese tea house in Kyoto around that time and named for the British royal family. Either way, numerous different brands now make Royal milk tea and in many, many versions: there are different blends of tea; some with creamy Hokkaido milk (even in the powdered form); even versions flavoured with cherry blossom, white peach or strawberry. The powdered packets have become popular for flavouring dishes, from cookies and pancakes to ice cream.

What makes Royal milk tea different to a regular cup of tea is that it's made by steeping the tea leaves directly in hot milk, similar to chai. Some people combine milk and water for this, but my mother always used just milk, as I do now. Use whatever black tea you like: Darjeeling, Assam or English breakfast are ideal. This is essentially a very milky, slightly sweet, not-too-strong tea and, when things don't seem quite right, it makes everything feel better.

SERVES 1–2

250 ml (1 cup) milk
1 tablespoon loose black tea leaves (or 1 teabag)
sugar or honey

Put the milk in a small pan and bring almost to a simmer (you will see it steam and tiny bubbles will appear around the edge). Add the tea leaves or teabag and turn off the heat. Leave somewhere warm to steep for a few minutes.

Stir in the sugar, if using (I am generally not a sugar-in-tea-taker but a teaspoon or two is a must for it to be Royal milk tea). Strain into a lovely cup (or two smaller dainty cups) and enjoy.

千利休の逸話

The death of a tea master

Tea master Sen no Rikyu, 千利休, (1522–1591) was an extremely influential person in the development of the tea ceremony. At the age of 61 he became tea master (and, by extension, a sort of advisor and confidant) to the powerful defacto leader of Japan, Toyotomi Hideyoshi. Hideyoshi, who had risen from his peasant roots to become Taiko – the absolute ruler in the Emperor's name – was fond of rather lavish tea ceremonies.

Rikyu became known for his very unique style of rustic simplicity and subtle wabi-sabi aesthetics (which he is credited for popularising). His tea houses were small and homely, with a low doorway so guests had to bow their heads as they entered. He incorporated Japanese-made flower vases, scoops for tea leaves and objects such as crackle-glazed tea bowls, which he created with a close friend and tile-maker, Chojiro. Hideyoshi so loved these glazed bowls that he gave them the name raku, meaning 'pleasure', taken from the second character of his palace's name, Jurakudai. This was such an honour that Chojiro's family took on this prestigious name as their surname.

Rikyu's aesthetics so influenced the art of the tea ceremony that they remain the style we see today. However, he paid dearly for his prestige and influence. Despite their closeness, the jealous and angry Hideyoshi ordered him to do seppuku, ritual suicide. Rikyu performed one last tea ceremony at Jurakudai, which is recorded in Okakura Kakuzo's *The Book of Tea*, where he gave each guest a scroll and then shattered a bowl, saying: 'Never again shall this cup, polluted by the lips of misfortune, be used by man.'

The guests left one by one, with the last one only remaining as a witness to his seppuku. His grave is at the Daitoku-ji temple in Kyoto and many memorials are still held for him every year. ●

> Tea is nought but this: first you heat the water,
> then you make the tea.
> Then you drink it properly.
> That is all you need to know.
>
> *SEN NO RIKYU*

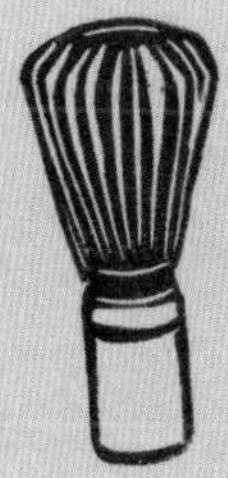

お茶漬け

GREEN TEA OVER RICE

OCHAZUKE

This can be as light and comforting or as flavourful as you need it to be; it is the perfect thing to make if you're feeling tired or unwell. It might also be part of a quick breakfast. My obaachan would often have just the rice with a little bit of sweet and salty tsukudani (page 110) and eat it with some pickles on the side. Other popular toppings include salted salmon (my cheat's version is to cook some smoked salmon), fresh sashimi, umeboshi or even kimchi.

You need a cup of freshly brewed Japanese tea here. You can use either hot or cold, and any kind of green tea – toasty genmaicha, comforting sencha, nutty hojicha or bitter matcha, or even hot dashi stock. If you go with tea, you really need the more flavourful, salty toppings to go with it; if you were to use dashi, you can add more subtle toppings.

This makes just one serving, because I think of it as something you might make for yourself when you feel you need it.

MAKES 1

185 ml (¾ cup) Japanese tea
100–150 g (4–5 oz) cooked Japanese rice (page 36)
2 slices smoked salmon
spring onions (scallions), sliced
pinch of toasted sesame seeds
dash of soy sauce
tsukudani kombu (page 110); umeboshi (pickled plum); strips of seasoned nori; kimchi; wasabi, to serve (optional)

Brew a cup of your preferred Japanese tea and put the cooked rice in a bowl (it can even be cold, as it will warm up with the tea).

Place the smoked salmon in a dry pan and cook for 2–3 minutes over medium–high until it turns opaque, lightly browned and flaky. Sprinkle over the rice, along with the spring onions and sesame seeds.

Pour the hot tea over the top and add soy sauce to taste. Add any extra toppings that you feel like.

玄米茶塩

GENMAICHA SALT

GENMAICHA SHIO

Here's another way you can enjoy the flavour of tea – make a salt out of it. Genmaicha, which is one of my favourite ever teas, is ideal for this because it already has a herbaceous, toasty, popcorn-like flavour from the grains of brown rice it contains. But you could also use sencha or hojicha.

This salt is great on a lot of things. Sprinkle it on roast potatoes or sweet potatoes, eggs (any which way), salads or perfectly ripe tomatoes, steamed fish or vegetables, or popcorn (of course). Paired with edamame it makes an absolutely delicious snack with sake or even tea.

I like a natural sea salt for this, such as traditional Japanese moshio or 'seaweed salt', which is made by the very ancient method of boiling seaweed in deep seawater over an open fire. This old technique has recently been revived, particularly around the Seto Inland Sea. As much as it sounds as if this would be a concentrated salt bomb, it's actually a milder salt that is rich in umami and minerals. It makes a wonderful finishing salt.

MAKES 1 small dish

1 teaspoon genmaicha
1 teaspoon sea salt

Place the tea in a suribachi or mortar and grind until you break down some of the tea leaves and rice grains. I don't like to grind this too finely.

Add the sea salt and stir it through (don't break up those lovely crystals). Place in a little dish and keep on the table as a finishing salt for anything you like.

中井侍の茶栽培と長老たち

Tea with the Nakai Samurai elders

Deep in the mountains of Tenryu, in Nagano, there is a small but strong community of 11 elders. They are the tea producers of Nakai Samurai, one of the small mountain villages scattered throughout this area that is 90 per cent forest.

As you follow the blue Tenryu river – the same river that continues to Shizuoka's famous tea-producing areas – you come across a small section where, instead of forest, there are manicured tea fields sitting on a steep mountain slope. The zig-zag path that leads to the top of the fields takes you sharply up 365 metres (1200 feet) – if we were in Italy and these were vineyards, this would be called 'heroic viticulture', where steep slopes, high altitudes and the natural landscape make it impossible to use machinery. Here, the tea farmers are not only heroic, they are also pensioners. The 11 tea farmers – who work together as an association and are responsible for the entire process, from hand-picking the tea leaves to sorting and processing – have an average age over 80 years old.

As we walk down the extremely narrow paths between the tea bushes and I struggle to keep up with Hama-san, who lives next to the highest tea fields, I wonder how the grannies do it, with their baskets full of leaves strapped around their waists during harvest time. The cat who is accompanying us sashays in and out of the bushes, while I try to avoid stumbling – it is so steep, it feels as if all it would take is one unfortunately placed rock and I'd just roll all the way down into the river. But the altitude and this spot – surrounded by mountains with the river right below – is what makes it such a special place to grow tea.

Nakai Samurai has short hours of sunlight, so the tea develops fewer tannins that would make it bitter, while the river below creates a thick mist that helps the tea leaves stay soft. They say the flavour of this tea is like gyokuro, which is usually manually covered with straw to protect the leaves from sunlight just before picking – the natural thick forests surrounding these tea fields and their position on the sloping mountain do that naturally. This harsh landscape, they say, is what makes the tea so unique and delicious.

The tea farmers here also don't use any pesticides or fertilisers ('we've only ever used fallen mountain leaves as fertiliser') because they want to drink their tea many times a day. It needs to be safe and healthy. ●

ほうじ茶ロールケーキ

HOJICHA CREAM SPONGE ROLL

Hojicha is a roasted Japanese green tea – the process of roasting reduces the caffeine, making this a popular everyday tea for all ages; it is even considered suitable to give to children before bed. It has a nutty, toasty flavour that goes well with baked goods, and I especially love it in this sponge cake.

I first thought up this recipe when imagining what I might make as a birthday cake for my mother. She lives many miles away from me, in Australia, and we have still never been able to share this cake, but I am positive she would love it. It's not very sweet, which is typical of Japanese versions of western desserts, but you could top it with more sugar if you liked.

I dot the cream with kuromame – these sweet, syrupy black soybeans were a favourite of my obaachan's and I always like to have them at New Year. They go well with the nuttiness of the hojicha, but, if you don't have them, perhaps try pieces of candied chestnuts, which have a similar flavour and texture.

Note that you will need two days to make the kuromame and you'll have more than you need for this recipe. They're delicious to eat just as they are, make a wonderful topping for soy sauce puddings (page 48) and also freeze well.

SERVES 6–8

3 eggs
100 g (3½ oz) sugar, plus extra for scattering
50 g (1¾ oz) cornstarch
50 g (⅓ cup) plain (all-purpose) flour
1 tablespoon hojicha powder (see note)
185 ml (¾ cup) cooled hojicha tea
250 ml (1 cup) whipping cream
2 teaspoons icing (confectioners') sugar, or to taste
3 tablespoons kuromame (sweet black soybeans)

To make the kuromame, rinse the beans and place in a cast-iron pan – this is important for their final colour (the iron has a chemical reaction with the skins). If you don't have cast-iron and you're not too worried about the colour, use any pan you have. Cover with plenty of water, bring to a boil, and as soon as it's rapidly boiling, remove from the heat and drain completely.

Add the measured water and bring back to a simmer. Cover and cook at a very gentle simmer for 1½–2 hours until the beans are tender but not splitting. You may need to top up with water to keep them just covered. Add the sugar and salt and stir until the sugar dissolves. Turn off and keep the beans in the pan until cooled. If you're using a cast-iron pan, leave them overnight to oxidise and turn jet black. If you want to store them further, keep them in the fridge or freezer in their liquid to avoid them drying out. (You can also cook them in a pressure cooker – just 15 minutes, being careful not to overcook them.)

To make the cake, preheat the oven to 160°C (320°F) and line a 33 x 23 cm (13 x 9 in) baking tray with baking paper.

Kuromame

100 g (½ cup) Japanese black soybeans
1 litre (4 cups) water
100 g (½ cup) sugar
pinch of salt

Separate the eggs into 2 very clean, dry metal or glass bowls, yolks in one and whites in the other. Whisk the egg whites until stiff peaks form. Whisk the yolks and sugar with electric beaters for up to 10 minutes, until pale, fluffy and creamy.

With a spatula, gently fold half the whites into the yolk mixture. Sift in the cornstarch, flour and hojicha powder, and fold in until no pockets of flour are left. Gently fold in the rest of the whites.

Pour into the baking tray – the batter should be about 1 cm (½ in) high. Bake for 10–12 minutes, until the top is pale golden and springy in the middle. Be careful not to overbake. Leave to cool slightly so you can handle it – although you want to work with it while it's warm.

You can do this next step with a sheet of plastic wrap, baking paper, greaseproof paper or clean tea towel. Spread it out on your bench and scatter evenly with 1 teaspoon sugar, to prevent the sponge sticking. Gently turn the sponge upside down onto your sugary surface and peel off the baking paper. With a bread knife, trim the edges slightly – to stop the sides cracking as they roll. Then, with a pastry brush, stain this side of the sponge evenly with a couple of coats of hojicha tea.

Whip the cream in a large bowl with the icing sugar. Spread over the top of the sponge, leaving a 1 cm (½ in) clear border around the edges. Scatter with kuromame, if using (save some for decoration, if you like).

The rolling part rather reminds me of rolling sushi. The tricky part is in starting the roll – the rest is all about the right amount of pressure (not too tight, but not too loose). Starting from one of the short ends, carefully but firmly roll up the whole sponge and then secure by rolling the paper, plastic or tea towel completely around it. Keep it like this on a plate in the fridge for 1 hour to set before serving.

You can add more cream to the top and decorate with more kuromame, or leave as it is, simply dusted with icing sugar.

Note: *If you don't have hojicha powder, you can grind hojicha leaves in a coffee grinder or pound them with a mortar and pestle, then sift and use just the fine powder. (With the rest, brew yourself a nice cup of hojicha. You can use it for brushing the sponge, or just to sip on while you're baking this.)*

抹茶餅

MATCHA MOCHI CREPES

My love of all things mochi was instilled in me as a child, thanks to my Japanese grandfather, Chodo. He and I had the same tastes, the same favourite foods. In most of the photos I have of us together, we are sharing food. Whenever we visited, he would bring special mochi and other sweet, chewy, sticky rice treats from his favourite shop in Tokyo. They were sometimes infused with mugwort and wrapped in bamboo leaves, or oak leaves, or dusted in silky potato starch which made it easy to hold the sticky mochi. It's no surprise that most of my memories of him are around the table at home, or in Tokyo, going somewhere to buy favourite treats. The only exception is when he wore his long white and pale grey priest's robes when it was prayer time in the Buddhist temple that he lived in with my obaachan.

These matcha mochi remind me of the treats I often shared with my grandfather. They are essentially little rice-flour crepes, that came about when I thought perhaps I could add matcha powder to sakura mochi. There are two kinds of sakura mochi, the more common come from Kyoto and are pale pink, sticky balls of rice filled with anko; the lesser known version of sakura mochi from Tokyo are little crepes made from rice flour, dyed pale pink and wrapped in salt-pickled cherry leaves. These, along with hanami dango (page 259), are a favourite sweet treat to take on picnics while you admire the fleeting cherry blossom season. Well, this green tea version is one that you can enjoy at any time of the year.

Traditionally, you would use shiratamako, a chunky glutinous rice flour, mixed with regular flour. The shiratamako gives these crepes their characteristic mochi chew and stickiness. If you cannot find this flour at a Japanese grocer, use fine rice flour; it will be a very nice crepe but have less of that mochi-like chew.

The anko recipe makes 1 cup (350 g), which is more than you need for this, but, if anything, I like to double this recipe whenever I'm making a batch. It freezes very well and I put it in smaller portions in resealable bags for whenever I have a craving for a sweet Japanese treat. You can enjoy anko with black sesame chiffon cake (page 228) or castella cake (page 158), inside maritozzi cream buns (page 260) or spread over the top of dango in place of mitarashi sauce (page 50). There's literally no occasion when anko isn't a good idea, if you ask my opinion.

MAKES 6

25 g (1 oz) plain (all-purpose) flour

10 g (½ oz) shiratamako or rice flour

2 teaspoons sugar

1 teaspoon premium matcha powder

50 ml (1¾ fl oz) water

vegetable oil for the pan

100 g (3½ oz) anko

6 pickled shiso leaves (optional, see note)

ANKO

125 g (4½ oz) dried red adzuki beans

375 ml (1½ cups) water

100 g (3½ oz) sugar

To make the anko, rinse and drain the beans (no need to soak them as they are small). Put in a pan with the water, cover and simmer for 1 hour or until they are so soft that you can easily squeeze them between your thumb and forefinger. (Or cook for 20 minutes in a pressure cooker.) Check occasionally that there is enough water to keep the beans covered.

Drain and return to the pan with the sugar. Place over low heat and stir to dissolve the sugar. The beans will release quite a lot of liquid, so you won't need to add any more water. Once this happens, blend the beans – I like a slightly chunky anko, so I leave about a third of the beans whole. If you prefer it very smooth, pass it through a fine-meshed sieve.

Return to the pan and cook, stirring constantly, over medium heat until you can draw a line in the bottom of the pan and it holds for a second or two. Leave to cool completely. This keeps in the fridge for 4 days or freezer for 3 months.

For the crepes, make a runny batter with the flour, shiratamako flour, sugar, matcha and water. If you're using shiratamako you will notice some lumps – don't worry about these. Leave to rest for at least 10 minutes (or overnight).

Lightly grease your best non-stick pan, then wipe away any excess oil with a paper towel. (It's handy to keep a paper towel with a bit of oil on it to grease between each crepe, these are sticky!) Place over fairly low heat – you don't want this too hot or the crepes will darken.

Use about 1 tablespoon batter for each crepe. As soon as you pour it into the pan, use the back of the spoon to thin out and widen each crepe to about 10 cm (4 in) diameter. Cook until the surface begins to look dry, then flip and cook for 20–30 seconds. These can be covered and kept at room temperature for up to 24 hours.

Use wet hands to divide the anko into 6 equal logs or oval shapes. Put one on each crepe, flatten a little and fold the crepe in half over it. Wrap each one with a shiso leaf, if using.

Serve immediately or keep at room temperature (covered or in an airtight container) for a day. Avoid putting mochi in the fridge – they become hard.

TO MAKE PICKLED SHISO LEAVES

I've made pickled shiso leaves to mimic the cherry leaves you find on sakura mochi. Simply layer the shiso leaves in a container over a layer of coarse sea salt. Add a generous sprinkle of salt over every layer so the leaves have salt above and below them. Finish with another good sprinkling of salt and you can leave them for months like this. Although the leaf wilts and perhaps dulls in colour, the flavour keeps very well, staying fresh and vibrant. Rinse off the salt before using and pat dry. These can be used for wrapping matcha mochi crepes and also onigiri.

花見だんご

HANAMI DANGO

Hanami dango is a very popular springtime treat, especially during cherry blossom season. The tradition of eating dango during *hanami* (花見, 'blossom viewing') has even given rise to a saying, *hana yori dango*, 花より団子, or 'dango over flowers', which can be read to mean 'function over form' or 'substance over style'.

Viewing spring blossoms to appreciate their transient beauty is a reminder that life is fleeting. Cherry blossoms are undoubtedly the most popular of the spring blossoms and these dango (the perfect snack for while you are viewing) are thought to represent their life cycle: pink sakura buds, almost white petals and green leaves.

Hanami dango date back to the 16th century. They were notably served in 1598 by the powerful ruler Toyotomi Hideyoshi (yes, that same bad-tempered ruler who ordered the killing of his tea master, page 245), for a lavish cherry blossom viewing party held at Daigo-ji Temple in Kyoto; Hideyoshi had 700 sakura trees planted for the occasion. Many people still have hanami parties, where they take picnics to eat under the blossoming sakura trees, even visiting at night, when the trees are artfully lit up.

My grandmother was never a fan of crowds and preferred to contemplate sakura quietly by taking in the wild cherry trees in the mountains. My mother's favourite hanami treat is sakurayu, pickled cherry flower tea, an unusual, slightly salty, delicately perfumed tea of salt-pickled cherry blossoms in boiling water. It is often served at weddings or engagements to represent new beginnings.

A note on some of the ingredients: the green component of hanami dango is usually made with yomogi, or Japanese mugwort. I've tried making it with local mugwort that I foraged in the Tuscan countryside, but it is a slightly different variety to the *Artemisia princeps* found in East Asia. For ease, I've made these with matcha powder, which gives a similar colour and an equally delicious herbaceous flavour. Another ingredient that might be difficult to find outside Japan is shiratamako flour – a clumpy, glutinous rice flour for making mochi. Use mochiko flour if you cannot find it.

MAKES 3 skewers

75 g (2¾ oz) silken tofu
60 g (½ cup) shiratamako or mochiko flour
3 teaspoons sugar
¼ teaspoon matcha powder
dot of red food colouring
ice

Stir together the tofu, flour and sugar to make a smooth dough. Divide into 3 equal portions. One will make the white balls – leave that covered. Mix the matcha powder into one portion for the green balls. Add a tiny dot of red colouring to the other for pale pink balls (start with a tiny drop, I use a toothpick and add more if needed).

Divide each colour into 3 equal pieces and roll into balls. Bring a pan of water to boil and cook the dango for about 2 minutes until they float. Remove and drop into iced water to cool. Drain and arrange on skewers, 3 balls on each, from green to white to pink.

Keep covered or in an airtight container. These are best eaten on the day they are made.

抹茶マリトッツォ

MATCHA MARITOZZI WITH ANKO

These delicious soft cream buns from Rome are a favourite of mine, not least because of their romantic origins. Maritozzi means 'almost husband' and these are named for the young grooms-to-be who would give the pastries to their fiancées.

I have always made maritozzi according to two great food writers: Roman author Ada Boni's recipe from *Il Talismano della Felicità* (1929); and a recipe from American Carol Field's *The Italian Baker* (1985), one of the most important books on Italian breads and other baked goods. These older recipes usually feature candied citrus, zest and even raisins or pine nuts in the buns; today you're more likely to find them plain. Also, funnily enough, neither of these recipes specify the use of whipped cream in the buns, but it is the way you will always find them in Roman cafes now.

The sweet fluffy dough has always reminded me of Japanese pastries such as cream pan, which are usually filled with custard, while the old-fashioned Roman pastries hold a neat and simple filling of slightly sweetened cream. This cream bun is also delicious with anko, like my very favourite Japanese pastry, anpan. The bitterness of matcha counters the sweetness and I perhaps even prefer it to my beloved Roman maritozzi.

MAKES 6 buns

1 teaspoon (7 g) dried yeast or 15 g (½ oz) fresh yeast
60 ml (¼ cup) lukewarm milk
200 g (1⅔ cups) bread flour
1 egg
50 g (1¾ oz) butter, melted
50 g (1¾ oz) sugar
1 pinch of salt

TO SERVE

125 ml (½ cup) whipping cream
1–2 teaspoons icing (confectioners') sugar
2 teaspoons premium matcha powder
2 tablespoons sugar
2 tablespoons water
6 tablespoons anko (page 256)

Dissolve the yeast in the milk in a bowl and add a quarter of the flour. Stir to a smooth paste – this is the yeast starter. Cover with a cloth and leave for 15 minutes in a warm spot.

Put the rest of the flour in a mixing bowl. Make a well in the centre and pour in the yeast starter, egg, butter, sugar and pinch of salt. Whisk with a fork from the centre outwards, incorporating the flour bit by bit to make a soft dough that's neither too sticky nor too dry. If you need to add a bit more flour, do it sparsely.

Turn onto a well-floured surface and knead for 8–15 minutes until you have a smooth soft ball of dough that doesn't stick to your hands. (Or use a dough mixer with a hook.)

Put the dough back in the bowl and cover with a tea towel. Leave in a warm place to rise for 1–2 hours or until doubled in size. (You can also put it in the fridge and it will rise slowly over about 8 hours, perfect if you're making this in advance.)

Divide the dough into 6 balls.

I like to use a 'pinch and pull method' where you flatten each ball a little, then gently pull the edges of the dough in towards the centre and pinch to gather. Turn upside-down so the seam is underneath and use your cupped hand over the top to gently roll the dough, pulling it towards you as you roll, over and over, to form a taut bun. You can use the palm of your hand or your benchtop for this action – you need a bit of traction for that taut surface.

Place seam-side-down on a baking tray lined with baking paper, leaving space between them. Cover with a tea towel and leave to rise for 30 minutes in a warm draught-free spot.

Preheat the oven to 180ºC (350ºF). Bake for 10–15 minutes or until the buns are puffed and deep golden brown on top.

While they bake, whip the cream with the icing sugar and matcha until stiff peaks form. Make a quick syrup by boiling the sugar and water in a small pan until dissolved.

When the buns come out of the oven, brush the syrup over the hot buns. Let the syrup dry and the buns cool completely before cutting open down the middle of the top of the bun.

Spread a tablespoon of anko neatly onto one side of each bun and top with whipped matcha cream. Use the side of a butter knife to smooth the cream. Serve immediately.

Note: *You can double this recipe, but don't double the amount of yeast: you only need 15 g (½ oz) fresh yeast to make 12 buns. If you need to use multiple trays, I recommend baking only one tray at a time, on the middle shelf of the oven.*

Continued ›

Index

R

S

T

U

V

W

Y

FURTHER READING

Here are some of the references from my bookshelves that I used to learn about Japanese pantry ingredients. I found especially useful and interesting an unpublished, incredibly detailed and well-researched manuscript – *History of Miso and Soybean Chiang* by William Shurtleff and Akiko Aoyagi, who have been researching soyfoods since 1972 and launched the SoyInfo Centre in California in 1976. They have a database of almost 100,000 references of soy documents and have written countless books on the subject, including manuals and recipe books such as *The Book of Miso*, published by Ten Speed Press in 1983. The collection of records, bibliographies and sources available on their website at soyinfocentre.com is a treasure trove that deserves a special mention.

The website and YouTube channel of Kioke Shoyu (kioke.jp) has wonderful interviews and videos of artisanal soy sauce makers and the Umami Information Centre in Tokyo has an excellent website on everything about umami, umamiinfo.com.

I used many unlikely reference sources, including poetry, literature and even films (I am a big fan of all the Studio Ghibli animated films, whose food references are often nostalgic and symbolic). I particularly enjoyed discovering – and finding an excuse to mention – medieval poems and 16th century books that have shaped Japanese culture. Many of these have been translated into English and are still available today. I have included them below in case you want to delve in.

John Gauntner, *Sake: A Beyond-the-Basics Guide to Understanding, Tasting, Selection & Enjoyment*, Bilingual Edition, IBC Publishing, 2014

Nancy Singleton Hachisu, *Food Artisans of Japan: Recipes and Stories*, Hardie Grant, 2019

Richard Hosking, *A Dictionary of Japanese Food: Ingredients and Culture*, Tuttle Publishing, 1996

Maori Murota, *Tokyo Cult Recipes*, Murdoch Books, 2015

Nakaji, *Koji for Life*, Nobunkyo Publishing, 2020

Harris Salat and Tadashi Ono, *Japanese Soul Cooking*, Clarkson Potter/Ten Speed, 2013

Shizuo Tsuji, *Japanese Cooking: A Simple Art*, US Edition, Kodansha USA Publishing, New York, 2011

HISTORICAL REFERENCES

Manyoshu, Japan's oldest and most important collection of waka poetry, compiled around 759.

The Tale of Genji, a classic of Japanese literature written by lady-in-waiting Murasaki Shikibu in the early 11th century.

Kissa Yojoki ('Treatise of drinking tea for health'), written by the Zen Buddhist monk Myoan Eisai in 1193.

Tenzo Kyokun (*Instructions for the Cook*) is a Zen manual on the running of a monastery kitchen and the symbolism of food, written in 1237 by the monk Eihei Dogen.

Ragionamenti del Mio Viaggio Intorno al Mondo (*My Voyage around the World* in the English translation), the travel journal of the Florentine merchant Francesco Carletti, who visited Japan in 1597–98, published posthumously in 1701.

Ryori Monogatari, or *The Tale of Food,* is Japan's oldest surviving cookbook, written in 1643.

Oku no Hosomichi (*Narrow Road to the Deep North*) is an important collection of poetry by Matsuo Basho (1644–94), published posthumously in 1702. The novelist Kenji Miyazawa once said of it: 'It was as if the very soul of Japan had itself written in it.'

Yojokun (*Instructions for Keeping Healthy*, sometimes known as *Lessons from a Samurai*), one of the most well-known works of the neo-Confuscianist philosopher, physician and botanist Ekken Kaibara, the 'Aristotle of Japan', written in 1713.

The Book of Tea, addressed to a Western audience, was written originally in English by the scholar and art critic Okakura Kakuzo in 1906.

About the author

Emiko Davies is an Australian–Japanese food writer, photographer and award-winning cookbook author. After spending her adolescence in China and studying Fine Art in the US, Emiko moved to Florence, Italy, and has called Tuscany home for the past 20 years. She turned to food writing and has been sharing her knowledge of regional home cooking on her blog since 2010. Emiko is a contributor to publications such as *Gourmet Traveller*, *The Kitchn*, *delicious* magazine and the *Financial Times*, and a recipe columnist for Italian newspaper *Corriere della Sera* and the online food writing platform *Scribehound*.

The Japanese Pantry is Emiko's seventh cookbook, after *Florentine* (2016), *Acquacotta* (2017), *Tortellini at Midnight* (2019), *Torta della Nonna* (2021) and *Cinnamon & Salt* (2022), all published by Hardie Grant, and *Gohan* (2023), published by Smith Street Books, which won Fortnum & Mason Cookery Book of the Year in 2024.

Emiko runs a cooking school and natural wine bar with her sommelier husband in San Miniato, Tuscany, where she shares her passion for seasonal, simple home cooking.

Acknowledgements

When I finally decided what format and theme this book would take on (thank you, dear husband, for helping me define it), I immediately wanted to go to Japan to visit producers who make these everyday ingredients, to learn more about them. The wonderful Megan Dung at Chino Tabi, the local tourism organisation of the village of Chino in Nagano, was perhaps as enthusiastic as I was about this book when I told her the idea. She helped coordinate some of the most wonderful meetings – making miso with Junko Ariura over a fire pit; with Ishibashi Tetsushi of Yaso tea, who makes native teas from the offcuts of the forestry industry; with the incredibly knowledgeable Keith Norum at Masumi sake; coordinating visiting the unforgettable tea producer Hama-san at Nakai Samurai with Yuka Naito and Habana Murasawa; and spending an afternoon learning about seaweed being turned into jelly in the landlocked mountain area of Nagano at Chino Fuminori's Irisen Kanten farm.

Thank you also to my dear friends Junko and Yuta Mizoguchi, who share a love of good food, have shared recipes with me, came with me to explore Onomichi and Shodoshima and act as interpreters. Thank you to Zenyou Tanakamaru, the executive officer of Onomichizousu, it was a very special experience to get to see the oldest vinegar factory in Japan, and to Onomichi Kakien for letting us admire the persimmons, my favourite fruit. I was very grateful to the Kagawa Fisheries office, who came to Shodoshima to coordinate my meeting the local nori farmers, Masahiro Hamada and Yuusuke Hamada.

Thank you all for sharing your stories and your passion for these ingredients with me.

Thank you to my parents, especially my mother, Sumie, for always passing on the knowledge and reminding me of Obaachan's (my grandmother's) sayings, her favourite foods, her healing foods, her Buddhist spirit. They have shaped me. Grazie, Marco, for always believing in me. Thank you, Hana, my sister, for your support and your eye. Thank you, dear Yuki, for your beautiful photographs and your perspective: I am so glad we could work together again. Thank you Junichi for coming to Chino and your photos of us making miso. Thank you to wonderful cooking teacher Yuki Gomi for first helping me realise that making miso is so simple to make at home and one of the most rewarding things I've ever done. I am hooked.

Thank you again to Paul, my publisher: I am thrilled and grateful to get to have another go at making a book that means so much to me, and thank you for setting me up with a dream team – Hannah Koelmeyer, Jane Price and Michelle Mackintosh. I could not be luckier. Thank you to my wonderful agent, Lou Johnson, for all your encouragement.

I had the help of a great team of recipe testers from around the world. Thank you, Lisa Brown, Sally Frawley, Sarah Benjamin, Suzanne Shier, Amy Wong, Sarah Slack, Trisha Waterman, Anne Bright, Susan Low, Gabrielle Schaffner, Sue Heward, Alyssa Vaughn, Peggy Witter, Racheli Herskowits and Ceri Jones.

I'd like to give a very special mention to some favourite Japanese food blogs, *Chopstick Chronicles* by Shihoko Ura, *Just One Cookbook* by Nami Chen and *RecipeTin Japan* by Yumiko Maehashi, as well as the YouTube channel Cooking with Dog, a charming video cooking channel by an unnamed woman known only as Chef and her toy poodle, Francis. These are the sources that I would go to for years when I craved my mother's or grandmother's cooking, or a dish from my childhood. Often, when I asked my mother a question about how she made a certain dish, she would simply send me a link to one of their blog posts, saying, 'I do it like this'. Thanks to these recipe creators (and others like them), who continue to share Japanese recipes in English, Japanese cooking has become accessible for many, including Japanese who live outside Japan and perhaps don't read or speak the language masterfully (like me). You have helped me find my Proustian madeleine and have inspired me to cook for myself all these years. ありがとうございました!

Published in 2025 by Smith Street Books
Naarm (Melbourne) | Australia
smithstreetbooks.com

Distributed outside of ANZ, North & Latin America by
Thames & Hudson Ltd., 6–24 Britannia Street, London, WC1X 9JD
thamesandhudson.com

EU Authorised Representative: Interart S.A.R.L.
19 Rue Charles Auray, 93500 Pantin, Paris, France
productsafety@thameshudson.co.uk; www.interart.fr

ISBN: 978-1-9232-3946-3

Smith Street Books respectfully acknowledges the Wurundjeri People of the Kulin Nation, who are the Traditional Owners of the land on which we work, and we pay our respects to their Elders past and present.

Publisher: Hannah Koelmeyer
Project editor: Jane Price
Design and layout: Michelle Mackintosh
Photographers: Emiko Davies, Yuki Sugiura, Junichi Miyazaki
Production manager: Aisling Coughlan
Proofreader: Pam Dunne
Indexer: Max McMaster

Printed & bound in China by C&C Offset Printing Co., Ltd

Book 413

10 9 8 7 6 5 4 3 2 1